# AWAKEN AMERICA

# AWAKEN AMERICA

## A Tale of Hope and Revival for The-People-of-the-Eagle

*Marjorie and Marc Caspe*

Writers Club Press
San Jose New York Lincoln Shanghai

# AWAKEN AMERICA
## A Tale of Hope and Revival for The-People-of-the-Eagle

Writers Club Press
an imprint of iUniverse.com, Inc.

For information address:
iUniverse.com, Inc.
5220 S 16th, Ste. 200
Lincoln, NE 68512
www.iuniverse.com

ISBN: 0-595-18886-9

Printed in the United States of America

*Dedicated to the America we Love*

*and*

*The Americans who will Love it throughout the 3rd Millennium*

# Contents

# An Introductory Alagory

## A Tale Of Hope And Revival For The-People-Of-The-Eagle

The-People-Of-The-Eagle were a fictitious Tribe, thriving and prospering for the first 225-years of their existence. They were a virtuous people, believing in hard work and ingenuity. They created new industries and new jobs, turning them into prosperity. So benevolent were The-People-Of-The-Eagle they voluntarily shared their wealth with others throughout the world, aiding those less fortunate than they with foreign aid as well as domestic welfare.

But then, just before their 225th anniversary something happened. Some say after 11 generations of the Tribe, a 12th generation had grown spoiled by prior years of growth and prosperity. They forgot just 60-years before, when their forebears had gone through 10-years of devastating depression ending only after they won a horrible World War between all their neighbor tribes. In their vanity, they thought themselves invincible!

Prosperity had changed their attitudes from thrift to consumption, from commitment to apathy, from vigilant to complacent, from trusting to litigious, from teamwork to adversarial, from creative builders to liquidators, from caring to self-indulgent, from studious to entertained. Changed attitudes brought economic decay to The-People-Of-The-Eagle.

1

Except for the very wealthy, individuals and their families went from prosperous to poor, from entrepreneur to laborer, from laborer to unemployed, from homeowner to tenant, from tenant to homeless, from happy to dejected. Their institutions for education, health, housing, transportation and caring for one another had declined so; they no longer had the will or the knowledge to stop the decline.

They had become so demoralized neither they nor their leaders were able to recognize what had gone wrong. Their leaders proclaimed if the Government Council took certain actions to manipulate taxes, tariffs and interest rates, all would be well. Each had a different magical combination for how best to regain prosperity and the Tribe argued about each, without questioning the viability of their leader's solutions. They didn't realize their chosen leaders were just a reflection of themselves. The Government Council's difficulties were but a visible surface sore on the deeply buried disease eating away at their vitality.

Suddenly, one bright sunny morning, a beautiful Angel-With-Large-Eagle-Wings swooped down from the sky and landed. The Angel encouraged The-People-Of-The-Eagle to be optimistic and not give up hope, saying:

> **A** rise you sleeping eagle,
>
> **M** ake freedom's message clear,
>
> **E** rase the curse of bondage,
>
> **R** everse this world's sad tear.
>
> **I** nstead of wealth and power,
>
> **C** onsider if you will,
>
> **A** world in which sweet liberty
>
> **N** urtures creativity, and
>
> **S** olves all kind of ill.

The Angel-With-Large-Eagle-Wings then met with The-People-Of-The-Eagle. In a large meeting hall, the Angel asked, "What do you think caused your world to decay so badly? "

The people on the right-side of the hall bellowed out in anger, blaming the Government Council and greedy labor unions for all the difficulty. They firmly believed in Voodoo economics from two decades before, during which income tax and inheritance tax reductions were given the wealthy so their money could "trickle-down" to the poor. During that decade the wealthy, as well as the Government Council, were encouraged to sell or borrow against the Tribe's assets of land, farms, timber forests, mines, skyscrapers and corporate industries. Overseas investors outside the Tribe soon controlled these assets.

The people on the left-side of the hall blamed the Government Council as well as greedy and wealthy property owners and corporation owners. They firmly believed that only by paying down the enormous debt of their predecessors, both public and private debt, could the Tribe again regain prosperity. They argued for both income tax and inheritance tax reform, closing trickle-down loopholes for the wealthy.

The people in the center blamed the Government Council and greedy overseas Tribes for their "unfair" trade practices, refusing to lower their side of the playing field as The-People-Of-The-Eagle had voluntarily done. If only they could get others to trade fairly and not take advantage, prosperity could be regained.

The Angel-With-Large-Eagle-Wings spoke, telling them all three were wrong! "Neither the Government Council nor any of those faulted had caused them to lose prosperity. Nor could any of them stop it! We can together find a solution for regaining prosperity but first we need understand teamwork is part of any solution and blaming one another does not build winning teams. All members of the Tribe are responsible, individually and collectively, because:

o It was The-People-Of-The-Eagle who were disloyal to one another at the wampum-register, the most important voting machine of all. Instead of caring about the prosperity of the Tribe's entrepreneurs and laborers, they naively forgot that new taxes for more police and prisons would soon wipe-out any low-priced savings at the wampum-register;

o It was their greed and inability to deal with risk that created their litigious society. This stopped innovation and development of new industries in all sectors except computer technology, real estate and entertainment; where both liability risk and environmental risk are low. Seeking risk-free guarantees on creative innovation, they stopped new technology sectors instead of accepting risk as part of life and trusting other's good-faith efforts;

o It was they who were so ill-advised and greedy for low-cost products, naively permitting overseas tribes to use "unfair" trade practices for over 40-years; destroying both the Tribe's industrial base and its high-paying job base;

o It was they who naively paid for their own Warriors to defend overseas competitor tribes against aggression, without charging those tribes for the cost of defense;

o It was they who demanded maximum quarterly profits, instead of investing in both focused Research *and* long-term Development of new industries (R *and* D);

o It was they who stopped being thrifty, making savings no longer available for research and development. Bingeing instead on consumption for frivolous overseas products, purchased by the Tribe on borrowed money;

o It was they who became adversarial, causing the Tribe to go into debt, instead of building constructive teams between industry, organized labor and the Government Council;

o It was they who permitted the family to fall into decay; without building family support values passed on to future generations with Common Visions about honor, humility, commitment, vigilance, sacrifice, striving, learning and pride in ingenuity."

The Angel spoke with affection for The-People-Of-The-Eagle saying, "The best solution for stopping further decay of the Tribe's institutions was to regain prosperity. Prosperity can be regained! It alone can put the Tribe's Warriors to work and swell the coffers of all institutions, the Angel assured them. The Government Council, business management or labor unions do not generate prosperity. Rather prosperity comes from individual people who create new ideas, new industries and new jobs. So don't worry about regaining those industries already lost. Better to rebuild prosperity with New Ideas and New Ideals.'

'The process by which rebuilding occurs in a democracy is random. Random efforts by individuals are better than programmed control by either the Government Council, business management or labor unions. Even innovation, appearing to come from a committee actually comes from an individual or two within that committee. Individual innovation in both the computer and biotech industries has recently demonstrated this with rapid growth.'

'A Tribe looking to the Government Council for answers will soon find itself believing in Voodoo economics. Voodoo believers are so committed to leading the good-life now and having "things" in their own life-time, they think it proper to sell or borrow against assets the Tribe had built or inherited from prior generations. Some foolishly believe they have no obligation to future generations. Others foolishly believe the Tribe has an unlimited supply of land and businesses to either sell-off at bargain prices or borrow against as collateral assets."

The people were startled! They suddenly realized they had lost their Founding Fathers' vision, some 225-years before, as well as basic values that had made them prosperous. An old Wise-Woman of the Tribe's Government Council stood-up to declare "The Angel-With-Large-Eagle-Wings is right." She poetically exclaimed to The-People-of-the-Eagle:

The objective of living some people may say
Is to satisfy ego through pleasure and play,
They go through their lives as collectors of things
Without thought of others hurt by their flings.

Our Tribe was blessed by people varied in thought
Concerned for their heirs and what hard work could wrought,
They sacrificed lives so their children were free
To live life in fullness with sweet liberty.

But the children of those who struggled and toiled
Had things thrust at them by which they were spoiled,
Without caring at all for the future it seems
They existed in limbo without any dreams.

Dreams are the stuff of which progress is made
To visualize breakthroughs for innovation and trade,
But incentive to do so requires acclaim
So people awaken to ignite the flame.

The Wise-Woman continued, explaining to the Tribe:

Our Tribe is plagued with four deep deficits
The budget is one that gives us great fits,
It causes our Tribe to borrow and pay
Depleting its ability to compete more each day.

Another is trade that's unbalanced severely
With an export of products unprocessed materially,
It causes our Tribe to lose jobs and profits
With no source of funds but selling of assets.

An absence of savings and profits invested
Stems from indulgence of self, yet untested,
It causes our Tribe to deplete its reserve
With no one to turn to in freedom's preserve.

The fourth is our families where an absence of will
Has caused loss of values the past could instill,
It causes our Tribe a great mental gap
As succeeding generations fall into the trap.

In order to keep from sinking our ship
We must begin somewhere to reverse its trip,
The only action to counter all deficits four
Is to loyally honor our commitments of yore.

Suddenly The-People-Of-The-Eagle awakened to the deeply rooted reasons their vitality was being sapped. They realized they had unwittingly entered a world-wide economy without first having created a world-wide political system. It was now clear to all they had naively limited their prosperity, following the Voodoo economics recommended by their leaders years before.

In order to create a continuous "rolling-wave" of new products and jobs, in addition to those in computer technology, real estate, medical and entertainment sectors, the Tribe's Founding Fathers had advised them to strive for continuing innovation in all economic sectors. They even wrote patent laws in their Constitution, encouraging and rewarding innovation and creativity by individuals.

The 12th generation chose instead to live off the assets they had inherited. Voodoo economists recommended they do this at the wampum-register by choosing lowest cost products; made by overseas laborers who worked as serfs, coolies, children or perhaps even slaves. The entrepreneurs who made these overseas products exploited this cheap labor, paid little tax and ruthlessly polluted the world's environment.

Instead of loyally buying products made by honest entrepreneurs and wage earners of the Tribe, The-People-Of-The-Eagle thought it wise to buy overseas products because they were priced at 90 percent of Tribe-made products. As overseas entrepreneurs paid serfs and slaves only 10 percent of wages paid The-People-Of-The-Eagle, and had few environmental costs or taxes to pay, the difference of 80 percent was theirs as profit.

This simple arithmetic enabled all The-People-Of-The-Eagle to understand how wealth and assets, once evenly distributed amongst their people, quickly transferred to overseas entrepreneurs with no allegiance to the Tribe.

The-People-Of-The-Eagle now realized how unwise it had been to make the Tribe's entrepreneurs and wage earners compete under such impossible conditions. It resulted in loss of industries, loss of jobs, loss of tax revenue and transfer of wealth to these newly powerful overseas entrepreneurs. They now understood why all their institutions, from schools and hospitals to industries and the Government Council, were struggling for survival.

Worse yet, depressed prices were making it even easier for wealthy and powerful overseas entrepreneurs to use their vast new wealth to buy the land, farms, mines, buildings and corporate businesses recently owned by the Tribe. The-People-Of-The-Eagle's greed for slightly less expensive consumable products was rapidly eliminating ownership of their most important fixed asset, land and vast natural resources.

The Tribe's childish greed for 40-years of low-cost products had caused more and more People-Of-The-Eagle to earn lower and lower salaries from overseas entrepreneurs, while paying higher and higher rents to overseas landlords. Members of the Tribe were even fighting one another to get jobs paying little more than overseas serfs' earned. Some even worked at less than slave wages, without any pay to support families and children. This occurred when certain wealthy entrepreneurs cut costs by scheming to create non-paying jobs called "interns" or by demanding extensive overtime work without hourly pay.

The Angel-With-Large-Eagle-Wings agreed with The-People-Of-The-Eagle that, indeed this was happening but they should not fear. "Fear of the Tribe entering into economic captivity by other tribes or giant international corporations, with a loss of individual freedoms and liberty, can be averted. Power and control must never be placed in the hands of a dictatorial few wealthy people. Anyone having absolute power will become corrupted absolutely."

The Wise-Woman reminded The-People-Of-The-Eagle that their Founding Fathers had warned them "the price of liberty is eternal vigilance." She accused the Tribe of becoming complacent, not vigilant, lowering the playing field to their own disadvantage. The Wise-Woman then asked the Angel what could be done to regain prosperity?

The Angel told The-People-Of-The-Eagle they could look to their democratically elected Government Council for leadership, but for solutions they should look individually into the hearts and minds of each member of the Tribe. The Government Council can readily provide continuity leadership, but new solutions can only come from individual women and men. Such warriors can create both innovation and a new Common Vision of the future. The-People-Of-The-Eagle should embrace that future. The Angel told them "in unity of vision there is strength," and then continued:

> This world is in need of far more loving care
> A love for the children who will soon be our heir,
> The children who will in the future it seems
> Inherit our spoils instead of our dreams.

> But how can we live without stripping our wealth
> Without using the total of Nature's great health,
> People today are in search of more things
> Unwilling to sacrifice though decay's in the wings.

The solution for all is found in Man's thought
A social technology for what can be wrought,
Cherish our thinkers, review all their dreams
And buy all those products that best suit our schemes.

A product designed to solve one of Man's ills
Is worthy of homage to encourage those skills,
Society's tribute should no longer spill
On the Tribe's entertainers and seekers of thrill.

Individual commitment is what we desire
For only such people can ignite the fire,
So seek out the scholar in science and thought
And ask quite succinctly, "What gift have you brought? "

The Angel said that achievement in life, for either a person or Tribe, should first visualize those goals and objectives it wishes to attain. Only a coordinated team effort can win sporting games and only a coordinated team effort can recapture the prosperity squandered during the past 40-years of self-indulgence. Recapturing prosperity will require both fierce competition and trust in one another. Envisioned goals can reach into the hearts and minds of the entire Tribe, causing them to act in unison as a team with Common Vision, each Warrior picturing individual tasks in attaining the Tribe's chosen objectives.

If The-People-Of-The-Eagle wish to withdraw from the world economy and become self-sufficient, that is a poor choice. Should the Tribe instead choose to continue evolving towards a worldwide economy, the Angel advised they first lead the way to their own democratic reform and prosperity. Then let other tribe's seek to follow their vision and ask to join them in a democratic political order, building prosperity of all peoples in the world.

Trust and allegiance to one another is absolutely necessary for any economic group to evolve and succeed, be it geographically limited or worldwide. Hence political commitment is needed before economic commitment can succeed. The Angel-With-Large-Eagle-Wings then proclaimed:

> Imagine a world in which harmony reigns
> In which people live without trouble or pains,
> A world in which all are committed to build
> By using each talent in which they are skilled.
>
> To cooperate as a dynamic team
> Does not preclude individual esteem,
> Competition between each person on earth
> Should be instilled from the moment of birth.
>
> To cooperate and compete at each instant of time
> Is consistent with nature and not out of line,
> People need to compete for material rewards
> As well as for praise from their peers as awards.
>
> Rewards are one's share of the world's total wealth
> Awards from our peers yield us great mental health,
> So compete for them fairly and strive for the goal
> Using skills that expand the world's wealth ten-fold.
>
> Participate fully in a cooperative tide
> So synergy yields results worthy of pride,
> But never lose sight of your nature as Man
> By striving to balance your life with elan.

Nurturing of the Tribe's people will be an arduous process said the Angel-With-Large-Eagle-Wings. Recovery will require a period of austerity and retrenchment, after the excesses of the 10$^{th}$ and 11$^{th}$ generations. But it is not too late! To which, the Wise-Woman responded:

> The root of our species is grounded some say
> In people who labor and toil for their pay,
>
> Others may claim that the strength of our land
> Rests with the rich who invest wealth as planned,
>
> The truth of the matter is neither are right
> For progress stems not from conflict or fight,
>
> It stems more from people who've been nurtured to strive,
> By institutes of learning that society provides.
>
> Of all institutions that nurtures one's soul
> The foremost is family to establish the goal,
>
> Institutions of learning are varied in worth
> But the family lays roots from the instant of birth,
>
> To motivate children to strive and attain
> Requires strong values about honor and shame,
>
> If awards for performance become apparent to all
> Universal commitment to prosper won't stall.

The Angel-With-Large-Eagle-Wings then told the Tribe, "Regaining prosperity for The-People-Of-The-Eagle requires shedding the false cloak of invincibility and once again competing aggressively for it. To do so recognize strengths and weakness, with courage and without fear, so certain very basic attitudes and habits can be changed."

In order to stop squandering their wealth by making overseas entrepreneurs rich, the Angel taught The-People-Of-The-Eagle about each buyer's "power-of-the-wampum-purse." The Tribe began to understand the driving force of their economy could be vocal and demanding buyers. With the Angel's help they created a Common Vision of an economic cycle where:

Buyers: Demand creative products, using their newly found "power-of-the-purse;"

Creators: Innovate new products to fulfill well-defined demands or create at their own risk and incentive;

Entrepreneurs: Invest domestically to manufacture new or improved products and fulfill well-defined demands, maintaining secrecy so these products can only be manufactured by the Tribe during a 2-year "rolling-wave" of progress;

Wage Earners: Provide high quality work in return for high wages, enhancing their lives and the well being of their families;

Government: Monitors and protects the Tribe against unfair or illegal activities, such as by protecting the environment to assure all manufacturing loops are closed-cycle and by having Tribe-made products clearly labeled:

"Made with pride by a ___ % Tribe-owned company, using ___ % Tribe-labor and containing ___ % Tribe-made manufactured materials," so buyers can make choices based on costs, quality and percentages.

And to finally close the economic cycle;

Buyers: Pay willingly for all domestic costs of:

    1) Innovative research;

    2) Development for domestic closed-cycle manufacturing facilities;

    3) Profit reasonably needed to justify investment risk;

    4) Wages needed to pay people for their time and high quality effort;

    5) Environmental protection that is closed-cycle within each plant, and

    6) Taxes necessary to support Government services and other institutions, sponsored and funded by democratically elected Government Council.

Before departing the Angel encouraged the Tribe to build a world economy, under the auspice of a democratic world government. However negotiating a New World order without having leverage is self-destructive, the Angel warned. Negotiate from a position of strength and fairness, he cautioned. Asking rich and powerful individuals to "charitably" relinquish their wealth and control is naive.

Trade barriers and tariffs imposed by the Government Council are not the answer, the Angel cautioned. Maintain open trade and competition on manufactured products *made entirely by* other tribes having democracy and wage scales consistent with those of the Tribe. But on products made in whole or in part by tribes having lower wage scales (say more than 10 percent lower), imports can be limited to the level of exports sold to that tribe by The-People-Of-The-Eagle.

This will encourage a continuing balance of payments with all Nations. Entrepreneurs, not seeking to limit their business volume, may have to start paying consistent wage scales throughout the world. This would raise serf's wage scales as they begin producing new products following the 2-year "rolling wave" expiration. The Angel-With-Large-Eagle-Wings then gave these final words of advice before departing:

> Be careful to resist temptation
> Voodoo economics can draw you in,
> Buy products that create innovation
> At the wampum-register you should not sin.

Be trusting of one another
Legal recourse is a poor institute,
Shake hands as you'd commit to a brother
Oral commitment's the best substitute.

Be sure to protect your honor
Bring pride to your family and name,
Ostracize any causing dishonor
Peer pressure's the best form of shame.

Be thrifty and save for your future
Invest as your mind thinks to do,
Risk's inherent so why try insure it
The best risk's when you bet on you.

Be innovative in all your endeavor
Creativity is the essence of Man,
Start new business ventures together
Risk all when the world needs your plan.

Be focused on ending world sorrow
But shape up your own act first,
By example lead into tomorrow
Help Democracy end human thirst.

Be innovative about democratic decisions
When representatives' vote too close to call,
On issues remote
Let good people vote,
So control is afforded to all.

Be global in seeking true harmony
Strive for a world full of peace,
Each family on Earth
Is the root of your worth,
They build values fulfilling your lease.

Be happy with one another
Seek joy in relations for life,
The intensity of living
Is highest when giving,
Especially between husband and wife.

The Angel-With-Large-Eagle-Wings then flew high into the azure blue evening sky and soon disappeared from sight as a tiny speck of starlight. The Wise-Woman asked all members of the Government Council to join her so they could think deep thoughts about what had occurred that day. They talked throughout the balmy starlit night, sitting near a roaring fire and envisioning the Tribe's future.

Next day the Warriors came out of their teepees to find stone tablets of writing given them by The-Angle-With-Large-Eagle-Wings. These were written guidelines for regaining and keeping The-People-Of-The-Eagle's democracy and prosperity.

In tender terms, the Angel's teachings focused on 17-New Ideas and New Ideals to help the Tribe build unity of purpose; striving to enhance their democracy and attain prosperity. All of the 17-Values were finely carved into the stone *Tablets*, including a Preamble, saying:

"I assure The-People-Of-The-Eagle that my spirit will remain with the Tribe for as long as it takes to change the Tribe's Common Vision to the '17-Values' provided on the stone tablets. These stone tablets present my loving guidance and advice on how best to 'AWAKEN AMERICA.'"

# AWAKEN AMERICA

## ARTICLE 1: THE EAGLE HAS LANDED

World War III started in 1974! No it didn't start with an armed attack. But it was in all newspapers when OPEC declared worldwide economic warfare in 1974. America's balance of payments suddenly became drastically negative with too many Nations. Since that time it's been a downhill slide for many of America's vital economic sectors. We have not yet awakened to being at war for so many years. From 1980 to 1992 the downhill slide was intentionally accelerated by political decisions, making America a debtor Nation borrowing excessively to create a politically false prosperity. Since then we've reduced that debt, but it still burdens us like shackles in limiting growth.

How did we manage to sleep through those years of economic warfare? It was easy! We were so busy "getting and spending we lay waste our powers" (William Wordsworth), in order to enjoy what we falsely perceived to be the good life. The downhill slide was clearly our fault alone, not that of our competitors.

They did not beat us. Rather we surrendered our economic and political power voluntarily. It was a voluntary surrender, a loss taken without much thought and a lot of complacency. Shedding that complacency, we can reverse the spiraling downhill slide. If we awaken to the urgency in all sectors of our economy we can regain technologic leadership in many sectors, just as we did in computer, entertainment and medical technology companies.

Retaining the pinnacle of economic and political leadership in tomorrow's world is within our grasp. Negative indicators can readily be reversed if we have the fortitude and strength to modify certain basic attitudes. Surprising as it may seem the same deeply rooted attitudes causing of our decline, as indicated on the ten-point list below, can be reversed. These same attitudes can become stepping-stones for recovering our position of strength and leadership. However this recovery needs a broad front consensus, throughout American society. Teams having Common Visions for success can readily coordinate individual contributions to our society's prosperity.

To focus on recovery, first requires an understanding of how much has been lost and how it was lost. This first Article starts by identifying "10-Negative Indicators of Decay," showing how serious our decline as a Nation has been. These "10-Negative Indicators of Decay" are only part of the price we paid during years of self-indulgence.

The press writes about decay regularly, referring to it as distinctly separate factors. Separate factors they are not! Rather they weave an intricate web of interrelated difficulties for our Nation, each playing on the others to create a downhill spiral of worsening decay. With Common Vision these can be reversed into an ascending spiral!

1) Self-Happiness Indicators: Self-indulgence and materialistic values continue creating a sense of loneliness for many Americans, not finding personal roots. Without family or friends they exist alone and insecure in a sea of people.

2) Marriage Indicators: Divorce rates continue to climb as couples find they can't find mutual happiness without fulfilling one another's basic needs for feedback and validation. Relationships are decaying without long-term commitment.

3) Children Indicators: Adolescents are becoming alienated from their parents as fear of the future causes them to withdraw into cults, drugs or simply into their room. This is aggravated by their perception of double standards abounding in a world that in childhood was perceived (and taught to be) idealistic. In adolescence this is perceived to be unfair at best or immoral at worst. Adolescent idealism has always been especially difficult for girls, having to deal with long-established dual standards demanding subservient behavior.

4) Family Indicators: Generations no longer communicate freely because they no longer function as a family unit, ranging in age and

experience. This deprives children of knowledge and perspectives necessary for planning and achieving in life.

5) Economic Indicators: Imports far exceed exports, but what is even worse, most imports are finished products and most exports are raw materials; such as coal, agricultural products and scrap iron. Were it not for innovation and creativity in the computer, entertainment and medical sectors, the national debt and interest on that debt would burden even more future generations. Paying down enormous debts incurred since 1980 both by Government, corporations and individuals is a high priority for creating prosperity.

6) Freedom Indicators: Businesses and land are rapidly being purchased by overseas investors, as more and more Americans work for and pay rent to powerful overseas multi-national owners. Freedom and liberty may be in jeopardy if that trend continues.

7) Business Indicators: As American companies go out of business or are purchased by foreign companies, the Nation is weakened by a shrinking private sector and tax base. We need to be innovative, creating a rolling wave of new industries as demonstrated by the success of new computer, entertainment and medical technology companies.

8) Job Indicators: Well-paying jobs continue to migrate overseas to newly industrialized countries, as sectors of our economy close. People continue to shift into jobs in the service sector, with its lower salary scales. Overseas owners are also in a strong negotiating position to get wage and benefit concessions at their new American plants, purposely located in depressed rural areas.

9) Education Indicators: Children continue to score at lower performance levels as both the public school and private school systems take on more disciplinary responsibility. This is due in large part to the family's loss of influence in motivating children. With adolescence, peer group pressures are replacing family influence. The resulting gangs, cults and drug abuse will be difficult to stop.

10) Government Indicators: City, County, State and Federal Governments are caught in a money crunch for more and more services not contributing directly to productivity of the Nation, such as:

   a) Cleaning up environmental hazards caused by past mistakes and excesses,

   b) Battling the war on drug imports,

   c) Bailing out banks and industries that failed,

   d) Barmaments,

   e) Providing a safety net for a growing number of unemployed and homeless people,

   f) Building and operating prisons for a growing number of unemployed people who became criminals.

Understanding these indicators and how they worsened between 1974 and today will require an introspective look. Our competitors did not cause our downhill slide. True, many countries became commercially and economically strong while we imported more than we exported to the world market. However the factors causing prosperity to decline were of our own making, hence the fault is ours because:

- We are the ones who set up manufacturing plants in overseas countries having low wage scales and low environmental standards, thereby exporting jobs.
- We are the ones who sold American research technology to overseas investors, in order to make quick profits, so they could develop the technology overseas.
- We are the ones who criticized our own businesses for making excessive profits and unions for excessive wage scales, preferring to punish them by buying overseas products. Such vindictiveness never had any merit because corporate profits would have been reinvested in new research or plant development and people's savings would also have been reinvested in private sector expansion.

- We are the ones who snuffed out our own industries at the cash register. Industries who dared charge a little more in order to pay a living wage to Americans, maintain environmental standards, pay taxes and make enough profit so investors could afford both new research *and* expanding of plant development (R *and* D) were penalized.
- We are the ones who went to the cash register and bought overseas products, to the detriment of our own industries and jobs, because their prices were slightly lower or their quality was slightly higher, or both. That was quite easy for them to do with their very low wage scales and taxes as well as minimal pollution disposal costs.
- We are the ones who permitted countries to export to us without accepting our manufactured products or services in return.
- We are the ones who chose to defend the free world against totalitarianism, without back-charging our trading partners in Europe, the Far East and the Middle East for their fair share of the costs.
- We are the ones who borrowed back what had been our own money, at high interest rates, in order to indulge our conspicuous consumerism.
- We are the ones whose managers ignored quality enhancement as an important element of production and consumer buying.
- We are the ones who voted to permit our infrastructure system to decay, from bridges to schools, without adequate maintenance or operational budgets.
- We are the ones who establish the most litigious society on earth, thereby inhibiting creativity and innovation.
- We are the ones who trained business leaders to maximize quarterly dividends, thereby limiting funding for research and expansion.
- We are the ones who take research breakthroughs and develop them with overseas labor and manufacturing.
- We are the ones who strive for power and the accumulation of wealth without limit.

# ARTICLE 2: WHY THE EAGLE BECAME GROUNDED

The objective of living some people may say
Is to satisfy ego through pleasure and play,
They go through their lives as collectors of things
Without thought of others hurt by their slings.

Our country was blessed by people of thought
Concerned for their heirs and what hard work could wrought,
They sacrificed lives so their children were free
To live life in fullness with sweet liberty.

But the children of those who struggled and toiled
Had things thrust at them by which they were spoiled,
Without caring at all for the future it seems
They existed in limbo without any dreams.

Dreams are the stuff of which progress is made
To visualize breakthroughs for innovation and trade,
But incentive to do so requires acclaim
So Americans awaken to ignite the flame.

Veterans of World War II must be "mad as hell" about how their generation's sacrifices and military victories are being squandered by their offspring. After having dedicated five of the best years of life to prevent colonization by violently ruthless overseas dictatorships, they must question why this generation of Americans is casually selling off the assets of our country.

Are their children and grandchildren so spoiled they are willing to jeopardize the freedom of future generations to lead the good life for a decade or two? Will they be the first generation of Americans to leave more debt to their descendents than they had inherited at birth?

During the years since 1974, we squandered much of our children's inheritance by borrowing to buy perishable products from overseas. While busy buying imported consumer goods such as cars and cameras, the people to whom our money was being sent in Japan, China, Taiwan, Korea, Germany, England, Holland, Canada, Saudi Arabia and Kuwait, were busy buying American land. Land is a non-perishable and appreciating investment having the safety of democratic laws in the United States.

What's worse is that wealth of America's middle class was transferred to a very few excessively wealthy people who realized inexpensive overseas labor could earn them vast profits. By slightly undercutting prices of American-made products their profit margins were very high. These profits were then used to buy American properties.

What better investment for wealthy people in Asian countries, such as Japan. Japan is a country with available land area only 30 percent the size of California and a population half the entire United States. Their only natural resources are lava from ancient volcanoes and educated people having an intensely agrarian heritage. Short on both resources and space for its people, what better investment is there for Japan than buying land, farms, mines and businesses vital to its economy?

It's logical for wealthy Asian corporations to buy coal mines for energy, to buy farms for food, to buy buildings for commerce, to buy Hawaii for recreation. By so doing they export their most valuable resource, hard working and technically trained people who contribute emotionally to their Common Vision of success. Although paying too much, these seemed wise investments to make until their economy crumbled due to too many such excesses.

Recent surveys of modern building ownership in America indicate overseas companies still have a controlling interest in many prime properties and buildings. Government estimates are that four percent of America's land is owned by overseas investors, primarily from Asia, Arabia, Europe and Canada. However that is four percent of our highest valued real estate, not including much of the Mojave Desert or the Great Salt Lake.

Of America's industrial assets, overseas investors currently own more than 15 percent. As fertile farmland is foreclosed or coal mines and hotels need an influx of capital to continue operations, be certain new capital brings with it equity ownership and control. In many cases this starts with a minority position and a seat on the Board of Directors. But as new cash needs arise, this small concession can soon grow to a controlling position.

Frequently, when a farmer or hotel owner runs into hard times, an overseas investor need only provide small sums of money to keep the cash-flow going. The collateral for such loans frequently includes an equity position, or an equity position in event of default. Such loans results in a quick-fix for short-term survival, but may soon have the owner going back for more. A three- percent overseas ownership percentage is therefore just the tip of the iceberg. A vast number of businesses, coal mines, farms, hotels and office buildings currently have overseas minority investors. They are therefore vulnerable to takeover in rapid succession, should hard-times occur.

For America, aggressive economic policies by our trading partners have caused enormous economic losses. America's predominantly exporting raw materials and agricultural products, while importing finished products from electronics to machinery and clothing. In New York the largest export is scrap metal. On the West Coast, the largest exports are coal, lumber and agricultural products.

What remains of our manufactured export industry is in large part made in America by subsidiaries of overseas-owned companies such as Seimans (German) and Matsushita (Japanese). By setting up plants in depressed rural areas of America, these companies obtained inexpensive land as well as wage concessions by using low-cost American labor. Advertising on television tells how these plants benefit our balance of payments and economic well-being. If that cycle continues American labor may be reduced to minimum-wage salary scales, competing with impoverished peoples both overseas and in America.

Borrowing and our debilitating balance of payments have weakened the dollar and caused America to become a debtor Nation. In the years since 1974, we transformed our strong economy and vast monetary reserves into a spending spree supporting our lifestyle and our insatiable needs for armaments, prisons, entertainment, vacations, water and power. We borrowed heavily against our assets or sold them outright to finance this spending spree.

But what happens if the spending spree ends and vast tracts of land are owned by overseas interests? Will we have maintained our most important commodity of all, liberty and the freedom to take action as we see fit? Perhaps not!

The day of reckoning for our liberty may be very near if we don't reduce our debt. It might happen first when Americans decide they want to clean up a pollutant or start a new armament program or build housing for the homeless, only to find that overseas bankers say "No, your debt-to-equity ratio is too high to permit further borrowing. "

What then! Do we wait until we lose our freedom of choice and wring our hands in despair when it's too late? Do we permit wealthier Nations to control our destiny? Do we let them develop technology more advanced than ours? Or do we do something now, before we become an economic colony of some overseas investor Nation? Take action! Gain control of our own destiny!

But how can we control our destiny? Are legislated tariffs and trade barriers the answer? No! Then what is? To find an answer concerned citizens must first identify the problem. Is the problem our World War II enemies Japan and Germany? Not likely! They never stopped us from freely taking action; they only competed aggressively as did China, Taiwan and Singapore. More likely Walt Kelly was right when his comic character Pogo turned to Cherchez La Femme and said, "We have met the enemy and they are us. "

# ARTICLE 3: COULD THE EAGLE BECOME EXTINCT

Our Nation is plagued with four deep deficits
The budget is one that gives us great fits,
It causes our Nation to borrow and pay
Depleting its ability to compete more each day.

Another is trade that's imbalanced severely
With an export of products unprocessed materially,
It causes our Nation to lose jobs and profits
With no source of funds but the selling of assets.

An absence of savings and profits invested
Stems from indulgence of self, yet untested,
It causes our Nation to deplete its reserve
With no one to turn to in freedom's preserve.

The fourth is our families where an absence of will
Has caused loss of values the past could instill,
It causes our Nation a great mental trap
As succeeding generations fall into the trap.

In order to keep from sinking our ship
We must begin somewhere to reverse its trip,
The only action that will counter all four
Is to loyally honor our commitments of yore.

How did Americans allow themselves to roll over and play dead? How did America become a grounded eagle in an economic sky-full of hawks? Only by understanding what happened would we be able to take corrective action. There is no useful purpose in blaming the hawks for having damaged the eagle; hawks have a rightful place in the economic sky.

We committed many self-defeating transgressions against future generations of Americans by developing many bad habits. Like all bad habits ours will be difficult to change, but not impossible if we can concisely identify each and try to correct it in our daily lives. Our motivation for change can stem from recognizing we are engaged in economic warfare equivalent to World War III, whether we like it or not. No less than our children's liberty is at stake if we do not reform our ways. The choice is ours to reform now or read about what could have been in some future book entitled, *The Rise and Fall of the American Empire*.

But today's Americans are largely self-indulgent and complacent. We look back at the history of our brief lifetimes and assume prosperity and freedom we have known will continue. Our sense of history and the transitory nature of prosperity and freedom are limited. We think austerity in spending and conservation of natural resources, in order to save future generations of Americans, too high a price.

The difference is glaring! World War II's generation of American women and men put their lives and families at risk to save democracy and freedom for future generations. Americans today are not even willing to do without certain "things" in their lifetime. We are addicted to gas-guzzling SUV cars and the latest power-hungry gadgetry for home entertainment. The manner in which we are purchasing these self-indulgent "things" is to borrow more instead of paying back past debts. Government, business and the people have a debtor mentality. Debt to overseas lenders drains high interest payments from our economy and sells equity in the most valuable assets we inherited from our forefathers, land and liberty, thereby denying both to our children.

The W. R. Grace Company had a powerful commercial message on television a generation ago. It was about a very somber trial of our current generation by some future generation of Americans. The message was such a difficult accusation for Americans to swallow, because the good life is so difficult to give up, intense anger pressured for removal of the commercial.

By selling off the land, we are selling off equity against which our children can build but—worst of all—we are also selling off "their liberty" to make free choices about what they wish to do, with whatever assets are left as their inheritance. Americans have a commonly held belief that future generations will automatically fair well no matter what we do today, and freedom and liberty are not at risk. Part of that belief stems from naivete! We reject any possibility of there no longer being any American owned companies and American owned land, making most Americans employees of overseas companies and renters of homes from overseas landlords.

If such a takeover of our economy were to occur, history clearly tells us not to expect overseas employers and landlords to be benevolent. That is chilling! Knowing first-hand the enormous nationalistic ego existing within countries such as Japan, Germany, China, Taiwan, Switzerland, South Korea, Saudi Arabia, India, etc. It's inconceivable that investor Nations who truly believe their own nationality to be "superior" to other peoples would not make life miserable for our heirs. The wealth in those Nations is concentrated in very few immensely wealthy and powerful individuals.

Nationalistic egos have too frequently taken the leadership of Nations, resulting in misery and poverty for the vast majority of the populace. Witness the recent history of Napoleon in France, Bismark in Germany, Stalin in Russia, Tojo in Japan, Hitler in Germany, Mao in China, Saddaam Hussein in Iraq or Pol Pot in Cambodia. To place our heirs at the whim of some dictator who violently takes over an economically and militarily strong investor Nation, or giant multi-national investor corporation, is to put America's future in severe jeopardy.

Even if the lending or investing Nation did not take away our children's right to vote, which they could, how free could an election be when employers and landlords are telling voters how to vote in the best interest of their jobs and their continued living conditions. That is a lot of pressure, which can sway many voters and result in a loss of freedom and liberty.

America's military might will not be enough leverage to prevent a loss of freedom and liberty. Relying on a future generation to wipe out its indebtedness by threatening military action against their lenders is wrong. It assumes our children will actually be foolish enough to vote for leaders who would launch a nuclear war and assumes we will still be a military power for wealthier Nations to be concerned about. Economic restraints may limit new military weaponry to those wealthy Nations alone.

In 1986, the idea of wiping out America's national debt and appropriating property owned by overseas investors was actually presented as a reasonable option for future generations by then Defense Secretary Caspar Weinberger. It was Weinberger's military budgets which tripled our national debt in ten short years. Wienberger wrote that future generations need only vote to appropriate foreign held property. That is an unrealistic option! It fails to recognize appropriation as an immoral violation of constitutional guarantees, creating vast economic turmoil throughout the world.

Only an economically prosperous and growing America can assure the freedom and liberty of our children. All other options are dangerous thinking and wishful thinking, dependent on the goodwill of others, rather than our own actions of choice. We have an obligation to our heirs to leave them a world of peace, harmony and prosperity; in which they are not economically weak sisters looking for charity. Let us instead be economically strong and ready to give charity.

# ARTICLE 4: STRENGTH OF THE EAGLE

Imagine a world in which harmony reigns
In which people live without trouble or pains,
A world in which all are committed to build
By using each talent in which they are skilled.

To cooperate as a dynamic team
Does not preclude individual esteem,
Competition between each person on earth
Should be instilled from the moment of birth.

To cooperate and compete at each instant of time
Is consistent with nature and not out of line,
People need to compete for material rewards
As well as for praise in the form of awards.

Rewards are one's share of the world's total wealth
Awards from our peers yield us great mental health,
So compete for them fairly and strive for the goal
Using skills that expand the world's wealth ten-fold.

Participate fully in a cooperative tide
So that synergy yields results worthy of pride,
But never lose sight of your nature as Man
By striving to balance your life with elan.

At the beginning of writing, 4,500-years ago, history began to record the deeds of strong warrior kings and their nobility. As a king's dominion grew, walled communities were formed for self-protection against other peoples. As these communities developed, certain land was found better for hunting, fishing and eventually agriculture. This greatly widened the scope of competition.

Now allegiance was owed to a king and his entourage. In return for allegiance, the king protected vested interests against other groups but did not relieve the basic need to compete within the group. Hence individuals found themselves in a more complex society with competition at two levels, that of a group and that of an individual within the group.

The history of these groups is well recorded by the manner in which warfare and competition necessitated clustering into fortifications, how the fortifications became cities, how cities found common purpose to become states and how states became countries. The driving force for combining into ever-larger groups was warfare between greedy dictatorial kings. Each king sought to be more powerful than a neighbor, in order to capture the fruits of victory either through offensive invasion or defensive warfare.

As societies became more complex, multiple allegiances were interwoven through the daily lives of people. Individuals developed personal allegiances in a rather haphazard manner, dependent to a large extent on the events of the time. If invaders were overrunning the land, allegiance to king and country was usually high. At a time of peace emphasis would more likely focus on self, family and community. Individual allegiances were always multiple, frequently made subconsciously and in many cases conflicting with one another. Each individual's selection of goals implicitly required evaluation of commitments at several levels, as listed below in an order of increasingly larger circles of people:

INDIVIDUAL COMMITMENT LEVELS:
1) Commitment to self
2) Commitment to spouse
3) Commitment to children
4) Commitment to family
5) Commitment to friends
6) Commitment to neighbors

INSTITUTIONAL COMMITMENT LEVELS:
7) Commitment to groups/clubs/gangs
8) Commitment to business/job
9) Commitment to religious affiliations.

GOVERNMENTAL COMMITMENT LEVELS:
10) Commitment to local community
11) Commitment to country
12) Commitment to Mankind.

For most rational persons commitment ranges from strong commitment to no commitment on several of these twelve levels. As each person has a limited amount of time to devote to these commitments, value judgements are made individually about the time and intensity devoted to each.

The intensity of commitment for most people will generally be greatest at individual levels, where there is intimate contact and direct self-interest. Levels of commitment typically decrease as groups become larger and direct contact is lost with the individuals involved. Hence intensity of commitment is strongest at the top of the list.

Most people think of themselves as leading a balanced existence between the two extremes of being self-indulgent (Level #1) or selflessly devoted to Mankind's well-being (Level #12). Each commitment a person makes brings both conflict and opportunity to their lives. Although we recognize an innate desire to be virtuous with all whom we have dealings, our time limitations compel us to first exert every effort to increase our own security and those closest to us. That is currently basic to the nature of human commitment and competition.

Balancing this basic desire for security is cooperation, which enhances a deeply ingrained need to gain the admiration and respect of ones peers. This causes people to accept community obligations, broadening one's focus beyond self-serving commitments to include mates, family, friends, social groups, religious groups, charitable groups, jobs, city, state and country.

The strength of America's democracy lies in just this mixture of individual commitment. Individual commitment to perform and be innovative, at multiple levels of society, rapidly creates a dynamic synergy. Such commitment only requires recognition of our own best interest. In a democracy it requires no Government action for people to develop loyalty and trust in one another. Rather it requires grass-roots consensus and peer pressure, encouraging people's emotional loyalty to a Common Vision of their better future.

Democracy was just such a Common Vision. America's Founding Fathers were the first people ever to rid themselves of a king permanently. It had never been done before 1776! The king of England tried again in 1812, thirty-six years after the Declaration of Independence, to reverse history. But the common American vision and allegiance, divisive over so many other issues between North and South, held the people together with emotional loyalty to one another.

Today the vision of consumer loyalty is weak in America. Consumer loyalty is unquestioned in Europe and Asia, because their societies are less of a melting pot than ours. Germany and Japan's homogeneous societies have no difficulty recognizing their Nation-family's well being as a primary political objective. Negotiating for an open trading policy with Japan or China is fruitless, because even if governmental doors were forced open the people provide a second line of defense called consumer loyalty. Disloyalty to the products of one's Nation is a uniquely American phenomenon.

America is a heterogeneous society, in part our strength to act and think as individuals and in part our weakness in losing a Common Vision of loyalty to one another. We became vindictive against American car companies thought to make excess profits or not creating quality innovative products. We became vindictive against American labor because of wage scales and featherbedding. These were immature reactions, hurting our Nation. Wisdom called for buyer warnings, restraint and austerity until wrongs were corrected. American buyers have enormous control of the economy when choosing to use the-power-of-the-purse.

Loyalty and trust in one another needs to be regained, regardless of customs or economic status, to prosper as a free Nation. Building trust and a Common Vision, we can aggressively seek to maximize one another's standard of living. To do so means choosing to buy one another's products, even though, they include costs for paying a living wage, paying for environmental controls and paying a reasonable profit. There is still enough wealth left in America to reverse the long-standing process of shipping jobs and money overseas.

To do so we all have a part! But the most important part is in our buying habits. For too long we ignored the 1960's warning to "Buy American! The job you save may be your own." If consumer loyalty can't be built at the cash register there is no hope. Every time we step up to the cash register we are "voting" for an American company and its employees or some overseas companies and its employees.

The American people can accept the small degree of austerity inherent in paying slightly more money for domestic products. By choosing American products, we create jobs and save on taxes for police, prisons and welfare support for those we put out of work.

Next in importance is the attitude of business executives and shareholders. If they can not resist the urge to maximize quarterly returns-on-investment by selling off assets, or licensing new technology to overseas investors or building new manufacturing plants overseas, well-paying jobs won't be created. American buying power can make these executives see the monetary value of the "new" American market for products "made in America by American companies with American labor." Without that vision and the monetary leverage it exerts at the cash register, the future is bleak.

Finally we the people of America can cease and desist from suing one another out of existence. It's possible for business executives to price products by anticipating the cost of wages, materials and equipment as well as the cost of environmental controls and taxes. However it's impossible to plan for the cost of litigation and its unlimited liability potential, wiping out not only profits but assets as well. No sane investor will place all their family's assets at risk in order to make a return from a lesser investment. Hence until the threat of litigation is mitigated it will be prudent for executives to continue investing in overseas manufacturing plants, where there is little exposure to liability.

In each society there is a vast majority who are law abiding, a small minority who will break or bend the law to their own benefit and a very few who are ruthless in their quest for power and wealth. Historically, but not perfectly, only Democracy has successfully kept power in the hands of law-abiding people who comprise the majority.

All other forms of government, whether the leader is called king, queen, prince, general, sultan, emir, sheiks or president-for-life (with or without the trappings of a pseudo-election) are dictatorships. Even if a dictatorship is thought to be benevolent, it never is anything but self-serving for the dictator. Dictatorship by any title is always evil because "absolute power always corrupts absolutely."

History teaches that a small number of ruthless people will statistically gain power more often than law-abiding and trustworthy people. This is because they can threaten others with death and physical torture. Hence power has historically fallen to the ruthless few; from the sultans and kings of old to the many infamous dictator/killers of this past century.

The small minority who break or bend the law are also more likely to prosper. They have unfair advantages, such as the mafia and yakuza with their violently gained illegal wealth or insider stock traders with their peacefully gained illegal information. Treachery is too often rewarded with enormous wealth.

The majorities in most countries have no democratic institutions or laws with which to fight back. They are slaves at worst or serfs at best. Only Democracy and the will of an alert majority can prevent dictatorship for long periods of time. Thomas Jefferson and America's Founding Fathers knew this when warning, "the price of liberty is eternal vigilance. "

But during the past twenty years America lost its vigilant majority. Democracy became reactive rather than proactive. Power was transferred from a majority of middle-class people to fewer wealthy people, many of whom were not Americans and had no allegiance to making America's institutions work. If this trend continues, Americans will no longer own the land or the monetary wealth and assets of our Nation. The American people were warned against complacency, but didn't realize how vulnerable they were. Supporting tyrants just because they oppose our enemies is both naive and a loss of vigilance.

For those in the American majority who wish to suppress greed and tyranny by a ruthless minority of evil dictators, there are three Common Visions for action:

- o First be vigilant and proactive about enforcing Democracy and the rule of law in countries that are Democratic,
- o Second be vigilant and proactive about exporting Democracy and the rule of law to others who do not yet have it, and
- o Finally be vigilant and proactive about enhancing Democracy and the rule of law in countries that are Democratic.

An example of complacency in enforcing Democracy and the rule of law is when we let people of wealth warp the Democratic process with illegal and immoral payoffs to political leaders or business leaders. It's equally as immoral to permit lawyers to create foolish courtroom pleas, like "Innocent by reason of insanity" instead of "Guilty by reason of insanity. "

An example of complacency in exporting Democracy is when we permitted Saadem Hussein to continue as dictator of Iraq after his destructive attack on Kuwait's oil fields. We could readily have supported free elections for the Sunnis, Shiites and Kurds so each would have a Democratic homeland. But based on "reasoning" against toppling a violent 20-year old dictatorship because it would "trouble" other petty dictators and kings, we chose not to set a Democratic precedent. That Saadem Hussein had violently grabbed power 20-years before and has tyrannized his people with millions of deaths did not occur to the American people or its leaders at that time.

An example of complacency in enhancing Democracy is when we fail to make positive changes in our Democratic institutions, but just let them wither and decay due to attrition (such as voter apathy) or corruption (such as political payoffs).

An example of a positive change would be if we modified our representative government to permit a popular vote on issues too close to call in the Halls of Government, nationally or locally. These issues could then be debated intensively in the news media and voted on by all citizens, using a telephone (800) number or the Internet. Americans already have unique Social Security numbers, making computer verification and authenticity as easy as banking or investing.

# ARTICLE 5: MAKING THE EAGLE SOAR

This world is in need of far more loving care
A love for the child who will soon be its heir,
The child who will in the future it seems
Inherit our spoils instead of our dreams.

But how can we live without stripping our wealth
Without using the total of Nature's great health,
People today are in search of more things
Unwilling to sacrifice though decay's in the wings.

The solution for all is found in Man's thought
A social technology for what can be wrought,
Cherish our thinkers, review all their dreams
And buy all those products that best suit our schemes.

A product designed to solve one of Man's ills
Is worthy of homage to encourage those skills,
Society's tribute should no longer spill
On mere entertainers and seekers of thrill.

Individual commitment is what we desire
For only such people can ignite the fire,
So seek out the scholar in science and thought
And ask quite succinctly, "What gift have you brought? "

For too long Americans have been myopic in our vision of the world, assuming we could maintain our position of leadership automatically. We locked ourselves into our traditions of lawsuits and unlimited liabilities, inhibiting both our creativity and ability to develop innovative new market sectors. To break this mold and begin an explosion of creativity, we can aggressively seek to make changes on a broad front across the entire fabric of our Nation.

To do so requires a Common Vision! People can not act in unison towards a common goal, without a Common Vision of the future and its impact on their lives. To evolve such a vision requires consensus about the values we cherish in life.

Such visions were clearly painted in the mind's eye of America's Founding Fathers. To develop modern visions and then modify behavior patterns according to those visions, will permit new behavior patterns to permeate the entire fabric of our Nation. These will usually originate from individuals, not necessarily political leaders, and then extend into both private institutions and Government.

Teamwork can result in creative growth and progress as well as a sense of pride in accomplishments. Because America is a heterogeneous society it's unlikely we can treat one another as members of a *national family*. Certainly not in the common cultural focus of more homogeneous societies like Japan and Germany; with all their commonly held values and faults.

But Americans are capable of treating one another as a *national team*, using a baseball or football analogy, trusting each other's goodwill and commitment to excellence as members of labor, business or Government. We can change attitudes and values away from get-rich quick schemes, short-term financial investing, long-term risk avoidance and liability reduction. Only then can creativity be unleashed on a large scale in economic sectors beyond electronics and medicine.

Innovation and creativity do not have to be limited to electronics and medicine just because they have low liability exposure. Unlimited liability places investor assets at risk, not just their investment. America has paid a high price during the past twenty-five years because of litigation fear, focused on suing for all an investors assets. Unlimited liability, liability extending far beyond invested risk capital, shuts off access to risk capital. It therefore prevents both innovation and creation of new market sectors.

The days of fortress America are behind us, when all competition was internal and the rest of the world just watched in envy. Today, what needs be done is to wake up to what has happened and rejoin the world-wide competitive fray. With courage and Yankee ingenuity we can recover what has been thrown away, our ideals and our continued prosperity. It will be difficult to recover valuable assets, as well as our economic position in the world. It may take several years of austerity and courage, not unlike soldiers in warfare. However voluntarily planned austerity, such as by going to the gas pump less frequently, is the best way to avoid what may otherwise be forced austerity in the not too distant future.

What we need do is change certain attitudes. These attitudinal changes need not be dramatic. To cut back on imports and achieve a balance of payments for instance, does not require a drastic change in life style. Simply by buying more American products of quality and reducing consumption, we can make strong inroads.

Recent American prosperity has enabled Government to pay back part of its debt, which by definition means it stopped the hemorrhage of borrowing that began in 1980. That is a good start! But the people could also follow Government's example and reduce their personal debt and business debt. It would be easy for families and businesses to reduce spending on luxury goods by 10 to 15 percent. This reduction in spending could include gasoline, which is our most vulnerable import product. By cutting back on spending for luxury items or by using products 20 percent longer, is not too high a price to pay on our children's behalf.

We can regain control of our own destiny only by paying down our debts, with both economic austerity and conservation at home as well as innovation we aggressively market abroad. We began to do this in 1992 and it led to a rolling wave of prosperity for some Americans, but not all. Paying off our debts permits prosperity to temporarily flourish but does not alone provide long-term prosperity. Our balance of payments are still too vulnerable with too many Nations.

Together with economic austerity, Americans need to conserve natural resources such as electric power and water. Conservation is a most powerful tool for controlling the supply and demand of world markets. Control of the demand side also permits America to control worldwide prices! If Americans can think and act as a team, emotionally committed to their Common Vision, not even an OPEC oil boycott or increase in oil prices could damage us seriously.

To correct our bad habits (society's addictions if you will) Americans can focus on positive attitudes. During the past years we have become masters at the art of making simple things complex. Life is meant to be lived with simplicity and balance! There is no reason to build complexity and intense pressure in our personal lives, our business lives or our Government. Striving for harmony and balance builds quality into life.

To again make the eagle soar, it will be wise to move forward on a broad front of attitudinal changes; ranging from individual commitment, to institutional commitment to Government commitment. The interdependency of these attitudinal changes means changes in basic values, forming a common American vision for the future.

If we can change from an attitude of suspicion to one of trust, creativity and innovation will flourish. As long as we fail to trust one another however, we lose synergy coming from the pooling of talents and resources in creative endeavor. Oral commitments and handshake agreements could once again be honored and trusted, thereby humanizing our relationships and reversing the trend towards legalization. Legal recourse is time-consuming, wasteful and traumatically costly.

Current attitudes are deeply ingrained. For most Americans, changing basic habits and values will prove difficult. Without new insights into why these changes are necessary, its unlikely people will be motivated to attain common American "Values" and a common American "Vision" for the future.

The 17-New Ideas and New Ideals presented by The-Angel-With-Large-Eagle-Wings had been orally summarized for The-People-Of-The-Eagle in the allegory tale about their hope and survival. The written stone tablets left for the Tribe by the Angel summarized those "Values" as advised for each of the 17- New Ideas and New Ideals, first in ***Bold–Italic*** type and then in more detail.

To make the eagle soar again, New Ideas and New Ideals can permeate American society, across a broad front of attitudinal change. It seems hard to believe the decline befalling our Nation since 1974 is primarily one of "attitudes" within society. But it is! Picture a new attitude of trust and creativity, based on long range planning and cooperation between Government, business and labor. Visualize an attitude in which Government, business and labor are all striving to enhance the Nation we live in through world-wide competition with other Nations.

America is rich in resources; the most important of which are our people and their ingenuity. If Americans can focus on correcting their bad habits and values with a "can-do" attitude and Common Vision for the future, there's no limit to our potential for growth and prosperity.

# ARTICLE 6: THE EAGLE'S NEW IDEAS AND NEW IDEALS

The root of our species is grounded some say
In the people who labor and toil for their pay,

Others may claim that the strength of our land
Rests with those who invest wealth as planned,

The truth of the matter is that neither is right
For progress stems not from conflict or fight,

It stems more from people who've been nurtured to strive,
By institutes of learning that society provides.

Of all institutions that nurtures one's soul
The foremost is family to establish the goal,

Institutions of learning are varied in worth
But the family lays roots from the instant of birth,

To motivate children to strive and attain
Requires strong values about honor and shame,

If awards for performance become apparent to all
Universal commitment to progress won't stall.

The New Ideas and New Ideals presented by The-Angel-With-Large-Eagle-Wings had been orally summarized for The-People-Of-The-Eagle in the allegory tale about their hope and survival. The written stone tablets left for the Tribe by the Angel summarized the "Values" advised for each of the 17-New Ideas and New Ideals, first in **Bold—*Italic*** type and then in more detail.

Each of the 17-New Ideas and New Ideals was presented in a consistent pattern of first identifying the weaknesses prevalent in America today and then presenting insights intended to encourage a Common Vision for turning those weaknesses into strengths. The 17-New Ideas and New Ideals all begin with the Angel's similar rhetorical questions, asking "What's wrong with America's attitude (about that specific Value) and what can Americans do to strengthen our Nation?" Response to each question starts by asking Americans to "*Visualize a new American attitude*," changed in what the Angel-With-Large-Eagle-Wings recommends as positive New Ideas and New Ideals.

The Angel cautioned that because each of the 17-New Ideas and New Ideals are intricately interwoven with one another, Americans consider a broad frontal assault on these deeply ingrained "Values." None of these New Ideas or New Ideals are stand-alone solutions, but together they can sustain America's leadership role economically, politically, morally and ethically.

| VALUES | TITLE | SUBTITLE: Weaknesses vs. Strengths |
|---|---|---|
| # 1 | BUYER LOYALTY: | Overseas Products vs. American Products |
| # 2 | BUYER DEMAND: | Complacent Consumers vs. Demanding Buyers |
| # 3 | COMPETITION: | Existing Wealth vs. New Wealth |
| # 4 | R&D: | Exporting Technology vs. Developing It At Home |
| # 5 | TRADE: | Weak and Dependent vs. Strong Negotiating Leverage |
| # 6 | CAPITAL: | Indebtedness vs. Solvency |
| # 7 | REWARDS & ACCLAIM: | Entertainers vs. Innovators |
| # 8 | PLANNING: | Quick Profits vs. Long-Range Plans |

| # 9 | LITIGATION: | Greedy Adversaries vs. Trust Between People |
| #10 | PEER PRESSURE: | Government Action vs. People Action |
| #11 | DEMOCRACY: | Corruption vs. Freedom |
| #12 | VOTING: | Apathy vs. Enhancing Democracy |
| #13 | POLITICAL ACTION: | Tilted Playing Field vs. Fair Competition |
| #14 | PEOPLE VALUES: | Material Things vs. People |
| #15 | INCOME TAX: | Inequality vs. Equality |
| #16 | INHERITANCE: | Values vs. Wealth |
| #17 | TERRORISM: | Passive Acceptance vs. Active Deterrent |

## VALUE #1: BUYER LOYALTY—Overseas Products vs. American Products

*By being loyal to American-made products at the cash register, by free choice, Americans can "vote" for domestic profits and wages during each purchase they make. When invested, these profits and wages will reverse any cycle of economic decline. Labels could be added to inform and encourage buyer loyalty, identifying American-made products and their American-made content.*

What is wrong with our attitude towards buying American products and how can we change it to strengthen our Nation?

A vicious cycle of decline exists in America today, feeding on itself. Like most cycles, it's usually difficult to find its starting point and even more difficult to determine how to interrupt the cycle, so decline can be reversed.

Like all vicious cycles on a downhill slide, it's difficult to break the cycle's momentum, stop it and build up-hill momentum. We can not ask management to do that at a time when many businesses are barely surviving at low profit margins. We can not ask Government to do that at a time when it's debt is high and the voters would not want Government control of the economy. We obviously can't ask labor or public interest groups to break the downhill slide, as they struggle for financial survival.

The cycle of decline clearly involves all "10-Negative Indicators Of Decay" listed above in Article 1. Each Indicator impacts on the others, showing a complex web of economic, social and political decline. On standing back to look at each cycle in its broadest perspective, buyer loyalty jumps out as both the single most pervasive starting-point for America's spiral of decline and the single most pervasive point at which Americans can interrupt the cycle and reverse it.

What did we do wrong to start this cycle of decline? From the 1970's through until today, American consumers have been vindictive, voting at the cash register for overseas products of all kinds. There is no more important voting booth than the cash register. It records dozens of votes each day, *for each person in America*. What is more, it collects money to emphasize the importance of each vote.

It served "them" right was the common attitude at the cash register, referring to American car and clothing manufacturers, without a moment's thought as to whom "they" were. As Pogo said, "We have met the enemy and they are us. "

Because we perceived profits and/or wage scales to be too high we purposely sought to punish other Americans who did not give us our "money's worth," by buying overseas products. We asked how China and Japan could ship quality products to America for less money than we could make it here and came to the conclusion it was either mismanagement, the high cost of union labor or both.

Our sense of family, as a Nation, was non-existent through those years. Without it we were bound to decline. Elected officials claimed it was their leadership in not raising taxes during the 1970's and 1980's that created prosperity. But to do so they were leading towards an abyss of indebtedness, far beyond any incurred for prior wars. The short-term prosperity was largely due to borrowing against or selling off fixed assets such as land and businesses. The handwriting of disaster was "written on the subway wall," but no one was reading it.

By the simple act of being disloyal to American products through the 1970's and 1980's, we denied profits to domestic businesses and created a "bargain basement sale" of America's land and businesses to overseas investors. Not to deny that many American manufacturers were blatantly unresponsive to consumer needs for quality and innovative new ideas; it was still too high a price to pay.

It was too fashionable in those days to criticize union wage scales or profits as too high or feather bedding as too prevalent. But shifting jobs to an overseas labor force was an act of foolishness by American consumers, again too high a price to pay. The price was especially high when we, as a compassionate Nation, tried to pick-up the pieces of people's lives. People living at the poverty level on welfare or in prison, present an enormous economic burden that continues to drain our economy. By transferring industries and jobs overseas, we managed to strain all our most valued institutions.

But that's only the tip of the iceberg. Failure to pay more at the cash register for American products only defers payment for our disloyalty and gets us an empty bag of groceries to take home for our efforts. The empty bag of groceries comes from numerous sources, including all "10-Indicators of Decay" listed in Article 1.

The state of decay continuing today in many aspects of American life is due in large part to our disloyalty to one another and distrust of one another. Perhaps we thought ourselves immune to decay, no matter how excessively we abused our institutions. We were not and are not!

*Visualize a new American attitude* in which buyers recognize economic competition (i.e., non-violent warfare) and consumer loyalty as actions similar to a soldier's loyalty in physical warfare. Voluntary buyer loyalty to American products can rapidly solve many economic problems without legislative action by Government.

The primary source of strength available to break America's downhill slide has been shown to be American ingenuity and our power-of-the-purse. If people commit—in advance—to buying products of value created by our innovators of new products, the downhill spiral can be turned around. The power of the purse has always been there. We just haven't heeded its value.

We can rapidly correct these cycles by voting at the cash register and buying American made products. It will not take long for American ingenuity to develop products for a new market of loyal American buyers. Whenever we go to the cash register to buy an American product we are very directly telling manufacturers what we want. If our goal is to buy status products having designer labels that impress our friends, those companies will thrive at high profit margins. If we shift our buying emphasis to functional products having high quality standards and in competition with one another, those companies will thrive at reasonable profit margins. Voting at cash registers dozens of times each day, provides greater control of America's destiny than voting in a voting booth once every two years.

Government need only give Americans the opportunity to identify American products made by other Americans. Accurate labels can be placed on all products and manufactured goods, clearly defining the degree of American ownership, labor content and material content. A simple label might say:

"Made with pride in America by a *_% American owned company, using *_% American labor and containing *_% American-made manufactured materials, by weight."

* Appropriate number for each product, so buyers can make value decisions at cash register.

This will permit buyers to come face-to-face with reality at the cash register. If buyers can discontinue their time-honored tradition of disloyalty to American-made products, prosperity will be ours. If we can see the bigger picture and insist on innovative American products at prices and quality levels reflecting reasonable profits, reasonable salary scales and reasonable overhead for taxes and environmental protection costs, American companies will thrive as new companies emerge.

Turning our *entire economy* into an upward spiral of prosperity will not take long if most Americans participate in a Common Vision. Participation will not preclude the buying of imported products. Each individual buyer decides at the cash register whether the cost advantage or quality advantage or creativity advantage overwhelms their loyalty factor to an American product.

The profit from American businesses, which is the lifeblood of our economy, can be reinvested in the growth of America's prosperity and not bled off to make other Nations prosperous. Profits and reinvestment of profit can be strongly encouraged both by managers and laborers. Peer pressure can effectively encourage conformance with a Common Vision, when that vision is widely shared.

No longer need Americans think of profits or wages as something to be minimized or eliminated. Rather they can be maximized to the extent value received and a competitive market place will allow. Peer pressure can be brought to bear on anyone who squanders profits or wages on luxuries, instead of reinvesting it in associated businesses or in monetary awards for creative people.

It would simply no longer be a status symbol to own expensive overseas products. Status will become viewed as purchases that support American creativity. A compassionate society such as ours is better served paying upfront to build its free enterprise system, rather than paying later and taxing the system into the ground for police, prisons and welfare. Either way we still get to pay!

## VALUE #2: BUYER DEMAND—Complacent Consumers vs. Demanding Buyers

*By demanding American-made products that are innovative and of high quality, buyers can direct the economy's growth. Direct purchases and a public information feedback system can define buyer's desires for the benefit of manufacturers and entrepreneurs, so they can more reliably develop new products.*

What is wrong with our attitude as consumers and how can we change it to strengthen our Nation?

Consumers have been too complacent and ready to buy what sole-source suppliers provide. When sole-source suppliers have captured an industry, such as Xerox, GM, Gillette and Kodak did, they tend to lose their innovative spirit. By supporting domestic entrepreneurs (even large companies can be entrepreneurs), such as Kodak, IBM, Microsoft, Apple, General Motors, Boeing and Polaroid respectively, competition and innovation can be rekindled by buyers. Loyalty to flying on American-made aircraft when scheduling travel, will rapidly encourage airlines to purchase domestic airplanes.

Today's buyers perceive themselves as the tail end of a chain-of-events making limited choices between products others innovate and manufacture. The perception of buyer power is currently limited to some 3rd level of importance in decision-making about the innovation of new products or improvement to existing products. Little perception exists about the power-of-the-purse, were buyers decide to raise themselves to the 1st level of importance and "take control" over direction of America's entire economy.

*Visualize a new American attitude* that considers rivalry between competitor Nations, the greatest motivator of all. As each competitor Nation or global corporation strives to capture higher market share they can motivate owners, officers, managers and employees to innovate:

1) New technology enhancements,

2) New ways to reduce costs,
3) New ways to improve quality,
4) New ways to service buyers, and
5) New ways to advertise products.

Hence the key to America's future prosperity is twofold. Not only can buyers make producers aware of their newfound loyalty to American products, but they can also "demand" innovation of new breakthroughs in efficiency, quality, product features and services. Buyers have the leverage to lead and thereby make American businesses more responsive and more aggressive. Buyer loyalty should be earned. Loyal consumers who demand more for their money will cause businesses to fulfill their demand.

Market pressures often breed success. Necessity is the mother of invention! It's the necessity of managing conflicting demands between buyers, sellers and subcontractors that motivates most breakthroughs. Pressure is caused by these conflicting restraints, and they are always in conflict, cause individuals to think and dynamically solve problems. The more positive economic pressure brought to bear on people (i.e., the carrot not the stick), the more innovation develops to meet buyers' needs.

Frequently this results in benefits unnoticed by the buyer, such as on time or early delivery. On occasion it may result in product improvement or lower cost, clearly noticeable to buyers.

This very complex interaction of people, taking on multiple roles each day, can not be predicted or programmed. It's random and haphazard in all ways but one, the regularity with which it happens. Random is good! It is the statistical essence of a free market economy, creating a continuing uphill spiral of successes by renewing both products and businesses over and over again.

As new or improved products and services are developed, everyone wins. The buyer gets more for less money; the seller captures a larger market share and makes more profit, as do suppliers. Capital is readily available for reinvestment, Government gets more tax money to pay for services and eliminate the drain of debt. The new wealth generated can rapidly improve America's balance of payments if newly innovative products become exportable.

Buyer demand can be made visible to suppliers of products, so suppliers have no ambiguity about how customers perceive their products. Only then can they be responsive, without risky guesswork about costly product enhancements.

To do this routinely it's only necessary for each product to have a self-addressed envelope, requesting a feedback vote form be filled out or e-mailed in after 2-months use. Specific questions about a product's strengths, shortcomings and specific enhancements desired can be asked in great detail. By asking the buyer what features could be enhanced, the seller can reliably go about the research and development necessary to bring it to market and make a profit. The vote tally can also be published as public information by Government agencies, so new entrepreneurs can access the data base and work to fill those market needs not yet filled by existing companies.

Buyers can participate willingly because this new system puts them in the driver's seat. Once utilized, the vote will effectively impact on all aspects of our private sector economy. Willing participation is surely a new attitude for Americans buyers, but then such new attitudes can enhance prosperity and prevent economic stagnation.

If the American people were to become demanding buyers, with a high sense of loyalty to products made by American owned companies manufacturing their products in the United States (even though they might be slightly more expensive), the following events are likely to occur:

1) Entrepreneurs are likely to innovate new products, starting new businesses and expanding existing businesses.

2) Existing businesses are likely to manufacture in the United States rather than overseas, thereby expanding plants and making them more efficient.

3) Environmentally closed cycles would reduce pollutant emissions to negligible levels, even though costly.

4) Profits would soar, resulting in investment for Research *and* Development (R *and* D) as well as expansion of businesses.

5) Numerous jobs are likely to be created.

6) Salary scales are likely to rise, in terms of real buying power.

7) People would have more money to spend, leading to more buying and more saving.

8) Motivation and creativity would be enhanced.

9) Social costs for unemployment, welfare, police and prisons would be drastically reduced.

10) Fringe benefits such as medical insurance and pensions could be restored by employers instead of having Government borrow to pay for a "safety net" program.

11) Taxes would be reduced in proportion to the reduced cost of Government services.

12) Families would be more cohesive without the stress of financial duress and needing multiple wage earners.

13) Divorce rates would drop.

14) Educational standards would rise, as parents could spend more time guiding their children and pay more for their education.

15) Drug and alcohol abuse would become less prevalent.

## VALUE #3: COMPETITION—Existing Wealth vs. New Wealth

*By gaining control of competition between American-owned companies at the cash register, American buyers can shift the focus of competition from capturing larger shares of existing wealth to instead focusing on creation of new wealth by innovation and creativity.*

What is wrong with our attitude about competition in America and how can we change it to strengthen our Nation?

Somehow Americans have lost their team spirit. Instead of functioning as a coordinated football team in which the linemen drive open a hole for the half-back, or a battalion of soldiers in which the first wave lay themselves on the barbed wire to speed the advance; Americans have developed an "every man for himself" spirit.

On a football field we would be picked apart! On a battlefield we would be slaughtered! Without a sense of team spirit, we become individuals seeking materialistic self-aggrandizement by grabbing for chunks of existing wealth. This is reflected over and over again in the daily press, witness:

1) Acquisition of large and small companies by investors desiring to liquidate assets and become wealthy, without building anything of value.
2) Illegal "insider trading" of stocks, stealing wealth and then bragging about it.
3) Tax evaders causing others to pay more, and then bragging about it.
4) Litigators seeking awards far beyond the damages incurred.
5) Savings & Loan bankers surreptitiously investing hard-earned savings in high-risk ventures such as junk bonds.
6) Lobbyists seeking Government grants for non-existing projects.
7) Government officials lying to Congress under oath.

Americans seem to perceive such illegal activities, as wrong-doing, but are too complacent to take aggressive action against it. People like Pickens, Boesky, Keating, Mitchell, Poindexter and Weinberger seem to get off with a slap on the wrist or a short jail term before rejoining society to legally spend their illegally gained wealth.

*Visualize a new American attitude* in which Americans seek more than self-interest, having broader goals in life. Goals including creation of new wealth, through hard work and ingenuity, are worthy of our American heritage.

The greatest source of new wealth is competition. It's human nature to respond to buyer demands in a competitive society. The ideal free-market situation is best exemplified by the computer industry during the past 40-years. Because of its negligible liability for doing harm to massive numbers of people, the industry attracted both investment capital and intelligent competitors. Computer hardware, software and support services became synonymous with the word "technology," as though there were no other technologies.

Other technologies having potential for unlimited liability, such as for environmental lawsuits, had limited capital formation. These technologies soon disappeared from America only to reappear elsewhere in the world where environmental regulations were less stringent. When the term "high tech" became synonymous with the computer industry alone, instead of thousands of industrial sectors, America lost vast opportunities for economic growth.

Each competitor in the computer sector felt itself under enormous pressure to innovate in order to maintain its market share. Not innovating new technology, higher quality, lower cost and better service was equivalent to suicide. Buyers and investors demanded such innovations by rapidly shifting allegiance to other suppliers providing creative breakthroughs.

Although in some cases the buyers had a direct impact on creativity by demanding change, in most cases it was some individual entrepreneur who suddenly appeared on the scene with a major or minor improvement to sell. Even IBM, with its locked-in marketing technique, found large sectors of its hardware and software business taken away by Asian-made hardware clones or innovative American competitors, such as Apple or Microsoft. Suppliers also served as generators of major improvements, as when chip manufacturers such as Intel made breakthroughs in miniaturization.

Demand by buyers can encourage and define the creation of this market-driven economy. New wealth, created by small entrepreneurs working from their low overhead garages, is overwhelmingly impressive. However it would be far less risky and costly if buyer's first indicated a readiness to buy products based on outline performance specifications. Once the buying market is known, both investment capital and brain power can be more efficiently focused on competing for specific markets. Basing these on realistic pro forma projections of market size, not yet knowing market share, makes the entire process more efficient and less risky.

Aggressive competition for wealth and the things it can buy is healthy. It's healthy at the individual level, the institutional level (such as in business) and at the governmental level. Complacency clearly leaves America vulnerable to a loss of liberty.

Hence a competitive spirit is desirable at all levels of society. Individuals can compete aggressively and honestly with one another within a company, to attain position and rewards, but at the same time they can be solid team players when their company is competing with another.

Similarly businesses can compete with one another aggressively and honestly but at the same time recognize they belong to a Nation-Team called America, and are therefore committed to buying from other American companies. The lowest price available should not and never should have been the primary criterion for purchasing decisions. National self-interest can always be an equal factor with both price and quality of product.

Americans can therefore compete aggressively without losing sight of the "balance" required at all levels of a competitive world:

- Individuals can compete with one another within a company and still act in unison and trust to protect the best interest of their company in its competition with other companies,
- Businesses can compete with one another within a Nation and still act in unison and in trust to protect the best interest of their Nation in its competition with other Nations,
- Nations can compete with one another within the world and still act in unison to protect the best interest of Mankind. All peoples have a common interest in the never-ending struggle to protect "Life, Liberty and the Pursuit of Happiness. "

Realizing dynamic change in Democratic societies only requires loyalty, trust and peer pressure. People can come together as a team, caring for one another. Only if there is broad recognition of how a team works in real life, can people envision their role on the team and act in support of one another.

## VALUE #4: R & D—Exporting Technology vs. Developing It At Home

*By insisting both research __and__ development be done in America; we can have at least 2-years of secrecy without competition before openly sharing new technology with the world. This would create a "rolling-wave" of exportable new technology. America will then maintain a leadership role both in technology and job production skills. Investment tax credits could encourage both new innovations __and__ new plant development / jobs.*

What is wrong with our attitude about R&D in America and how can we change it to strengthen our Nation?

Our weakness is in not investing in research and development (R&D), which has been the backbone of America's prosperity since Edison, Bell and Ford. Most large companies can trace their roots back to an innovative person (a single individual). But once OPEC was formed in 1974, and the oil shortage began to drain profitability, R&D was cut from most American companies budgets, never to return. Even those few companies having research budgets, find that development of manufacturing is later moved overseas for cheap labor. Doing research and then giving away development rights is a waste of Yankee ingenuity.

We can restructure funding so private sector companies and individual entrepreneurs, not just universities and Government think tanks, are deeply involved in R&D. The entrepreneurial spirit of individual Americans will rapidly re-emerge. Individuals and small private sector companies are closest to the pulse of the market but are today without funding (in large part due to the impact of our litigious society and its focus on quick quarterly profits).

Funding is needed for both research *and* development of products; so well-paying jobs do not continue to emigrate overseas. As exemplified by the executive who researched a product in America but faced enormous pressures to either sell it or develop it overseas, high paying industrial jobs continue being taken away from the American people.

In the construction industry, where firm-specific know-how provided the cutting edge for getting overseas contracts for decades, labor intensive contracts have dwindled from a mighty river of overseas exports and jobs to a steady stream of overseas imports. We now have Japanese, German and Korean contractors doing more and more work in the United States, with U. S. contractors doing very little work throughout the world.

In large part this is due to our failure in maintaining R&D leadership. An example is when a Japanese contractor easily won a profitable tunnel contract in San Francisco because it had built a new tunneling machine. Or when new technology for earthquake protection of buildings and bridges—invented in America 30-years ago and proven on University shake-table tests to be truly earthquake-proof—still can't be used. Liability laws in America *totally prevent* construction of any buildings or bridges with new earthquake-proof technology. Even with so many people's lives and so much property at risk, unlimited liability makes earthquake-proof technology too risky an investment because even the smallest possibility of anything going wrong places *all of the investor's assets* at risk to lawsuits by injured plaintiffs. Only when continuing the same old technology that failed so many times before, does current American law protect investors and owners saying, "It was an act of God, so no one is liable."

Many current retrofit projects could be completed to an earthquake-proof standard, at a cost to taxpayers of only 15-percent their currently astronomical budgets. These include all the San Francisco Bay and San Diego Bay Bridge crossings, Freeway bridge crossings, commercial office buildings as well as such massive buildings as City Halls and Hospitals throughout the Western States and Midwestern States. So the new technology remains proven on laboratory shaking-table tests but too risky to use, simply because no one has used it before and no one of wealth is willing to risk their assets going first. Even the U.S. Army and Navy have not had the courage to go first, with Admirals and Generals saying it's not their role to innovate and "go first" with anything other than weapons systems.

In the U. S. construction industry, not even the largest companies had any R&D budget last year, while trying to compete with larger Japanese and German construction companies having annual R&D investments greater than 1 percent of their total revenue. Such enormous reinvestment levels have funded new private sector research facilities, giving overseas competitors a major marketing and performance advantage.

*Visualize a new American attitude* in which American executives and entrepreneurs, in return for buyer loyalty, commit to the development of new domestic manufacturing plants in order to create new jobs and train Americans in new technology skills. The focus can be on new or modified products, rapidly placed on the market. This means the lion's share of funds would go to development rather than basic research, so those products already close to commercial reality can begin to generate capital and jobs.

R&D means research *and* development. It is not sufficient to perform research, then export development to countries having cheap labor and low environmental standards. These countries can of course price products below domestic manufacturers, putting Americans out of business. By exporting jobs, we reduce our standard of living and exacerbate social costs, leading to another vicious cycle of higher taxes.

To say creativity is dead in America is a bit too strong. Certainly it's alive and well in the software and entertainment industries because with no tangible products involved, the risk of litigation and unlimited liability are low. Creativity also exists in defense/space industries (including the electronics industry) because of the vast infusion of tax dollars and the fact our Federal Government never sues private companies. Other than these two industries, risk-taking for development in America is limited to low-risk investments like real estate, having little or no liability for injury to 3rd parties. Even the medical industry, with its vast success in researching new products in America, transfers ownership capital and manufacturing assets overseas. This puts them out of reach of litigious America's unlimited liability laws.

Legislation is therefore needed to "hold harmless" or "limit liability" for American companies and individuals willing to be first in implementing new technology manufactured in America. Without such legislated protection, progress will continue to stall in any new technology having even a low possibility of unlimited liability.

America's citizenry has the power to encourage an out-pouring of new products and jobs, based on Yankee ingenuity. We can simply commit in advance to buying new products when they reach market. We can encourage profitability and reinvestment of profit, particularly when invested in the same businesses making the profit. In a free enterprise system, profit can create cycles of growth leading to new jobs and prosperity. Money is far better spent at the cash register buying American products—priced to include high profits and a living wage—than paying taxes to support people on unemployment and welfare or in prison. Only companies with high profit margins can afford research and development.

Government can encourage investments in research, but major investment tax credits can be reserved for new development and existing plant modernization. Innovative products evolved can have self-contained control over disposal of all toxic effluents. This too presents a creative challenge, developing cost-effective in-plant disposal systems, so we can compete with countries having little concern for toxic dumping in the oceans or skies. Now that smokestack industries, our heaviest polluters, have been transferred to overseas island Nations such as Taiwan, Japan and Malaysia, where they can dump indiscriminately into the sea or sky; our new products seem to have far less pollution.

All environmental concerns can be addressed, so resources are conserved and reused to the greatest extent possible. Conservation of resources and reduction in pollution are totally compatible concepts for worldwide export. We can provide such leadership, especially now that traces of toxic lead from Japanese industries have been identified off the coast of California. It's apparently too small a world to lose control of our waste streams.

We might not try recovering the old smokestack industries, such as steel making and cement. These high pollution industries are not only unrecoverable but are most likely unwanted. Their pollution load was too much and too concentrated in America during the first half of the 20th Century. It's far better to have them spread out and diluted around the world.

Americans can also welcome creativity on service oriented breakthroughs which export technology. Science and art have little negative environmental impact. However the exporting of such breakthroughs can be timed to a 2-year "rolling wave" of production here in America, before being exported. Our foremost objective can be to create high-paying value-added jobs for Americans, so prosperity spreads overseas *after* it's well-established here.

As we develop new innovations, let the rest of the world follow our lead, not only in technology but in the social, artistic and political fields as well. If we can maintain a 2-year "rolling-wave" head start on the rest of the world (new innovations rolling in to replace exported technology that is two or more years old), it will result in full employment with people earning a living wage. Welfare and unemployment costs will be drastically reduced and prison costs will decline. People will have meaningful jobs, instilling dignity to the family and encouraging individual creativity.

If each new product has a planned development in which the first 2-years of production is done in America by Americans, it will provide the jobs that provide the wages that permit Americans to "Buy American." It will also permit Americans to be at the forefront of a 2-year "rolling wave" of technology and production. Being on the forefront will feed on itself, as people in all walks of life contribute their ideas and energies to improve product lines and their delivery systems.

After 2-years, product manufacture overseas can be acceptable as America moves on to the continuing evolution of new innovations enriching the lives of people everywhere. Trade can be free and open with all

Nations, except for the broad limitations of "Buying American," maintaining a positive trade balance each quarter and retaining up to a 2-year lead on all new technologies.

Of course other countries can be expected to adopt the same or similar policies, leading to healthy worldwide innovation and competition. America can rely on good-old-fashioned "Yankee ingenuity" to compete successfully, encouraging other Nations to either join us in competition or join us in political unity as a Democracy of people.

This can only be achieved if Americans again compete aggressively and creatively. Prosperity and growth of export products and services will permit us to market our 2-year technology lead overseas. It will also affirm America's leadership role into the 21st Century.

## VALUE #5: TRADE—Weak and Dependent vs. Strong Negotiating Leverage

*Maintain open trade and competition on manufactured products, made entirely by other Nations having democracy and wage scales consistent with those of America. But on products made in whole or in part by Nations having lower wage scales (say more than 10 percent lower), imports can be limited to the level of exports sold to that Nation by America. This will limit our quarterly imports from such Nations to a dollar amount no more than 10-percent of their imports from us, providing a balance of payments without unfair trade barriers or tariffs. Creating a level playing field for international competition.*

What is wrong with our attitude about America's trade imbalance and national debt, and how can we change it to strengthen our Nation?

Our weakness is in complacency, having lost the instinct to compete aggressively with other Nations. Our society has gone soft with "getting and spending" by selling off its assets or borrowing against its assets. Our Nation's assets have a tangible limit. To reverse this trend will require courage to return to austerity, emphasizing people, team-oriented values and a renewed commitment to creativity and competition.

If Americans were alert to the rapid draining of their economic and political strength, they would not be complacent about borrowing from overseas banks to buy imported products. They might be more conscious about conserving natural resources, particularly oil and gas products eating so heavily into our imbalance of payments and contributing so strongly to our national debt. Voluntary austerity, to reduce usage and conserve resources, would go a long way to solving our economic problems.

Complacency also prevails in our trade negotiations with other Nations. These negotiations could be based on a high degree of leverage. No longer can we let Japan continue its word games built around a time-honored Japanese tradition of "tatemei" (this is what I say) and "honne" (this is what I mean). For too many decades we tried to negotiate with Japan without understanding this Japanese tradition, which when translated into English is confusing double-speak.

Only with the untimely passing of Secretary of Commerce Malcolm Baldridge at a California rodeo in 1987 did the Reagan administration get a Secretary of Commerce who began to stand up to the Nakasone word-game. We have for too many years been accepting Japan and China's self-serving position of limiting trade within its borders but audaciously insisting on free trade elsewhere in the world.

It was almost humorous (with the right amount of pathos) to watch Nakasone promise to open up Japan to American products, even simple agricultural products such as oranges. He would then go back to Japan and four months later issue a worldwide press release showing Japanese orange growers burning Uncle Sam in effigy. Nakasone would then come back two months later to apologize for not being able to politically accomplish the task. And we accepted that over and over again. Whose fault is that, the Japanese who continued to reap the harvest from both sides of the negotiation or ourselves for being naive and not competing aggressively or buying wisely?

*Visualize a new American attitude* in which Americans participate in and enjoy economic competition. Economic competition can be a great source of national pride, without war. It's even entertaining and deeply pleasurable when victories are at hand in which everyone wins, such as by creating new products or solving major problems for Mankind. Innovations create both jobs and export sales.

Even Government can adopt an aggressive and competitive stance with respect to other Nations. Government complacency through the 1980's permitted other Nations to negotiate free and unlimited access to our markets while theirs remained closed. The tilted playing field was complacency and naivete at its worst. It was tilted the wrong way! This error in judgement encouraged large trade imbalances and drained capital from our economy, making us the largest debtor Nation in the world and putting real assets (land and businesses) at risk.

To correct that error, Government can rapidly stop the hemorrhaging by legislation causing all countries to buy products from America in dollar amounts that are closely equal to the dollar amounts they propose to export to us each quarter. We could maintain open trade and competition on manufactured products *made entirely by* Nations having wage scales consistent with those of America. But on products made in whole or in part by Nations having lower wage scales (say more than 10-percent lower), imports can be limited to the level of exports sold to that Nation each month. Although this may require a transition period of a year or more to achieve without inordinate disruption, after 12 to 36-months our balance of payments might never again be negative with *any* Nation.

This will encourage a continuing balance of payments with all Nations. Entrepreneurs paying low wages, but not seeking to limit their business volume, may then begin to pay wage scales consistent throughout the world. This may effectively equalize wage scales and lead dictatorships into Democracy.

The results of such legislation might cause some disruption and hardship. Government can help industry through the transition, such as by funding an American businessman who sold cars made in Germany but now chooses to withdraw from that market. As for the loss of imported luxury items, austerity is sometimes the price of eternal vigilance.

In addition to investment tax credits for developing new technology in America, export tax credits can be additive so new technology is focused on overseas markets. Only by exporting more and more products can we afford to participate fully in the evolving world economy.

The primary result of a balanced trade policy will be to regain leverage in dealing with our trading partners. By competing aggressively, in our own best interest as a Nation, we will encourage other Nations to purchase more American products or voluntarily cut back on certain products they export to us. If they elect to buy more it will create additional well-paying

American jobs. If they elect to export less, which is doubt, we will have to learn to do without certain options in our lives.

However that's a small price to pay, for only a short period of time. As American companies move to fill the market voids left by overseas competitors, they will create more well-paying American jobs. If overseas companies elect to open manufacturing plants in America, creating new jobs for Americans, all imported equipment and materials delivered to that plant would be counted in the Nation-to-Nation balance of payments.

No more the grounded eagle but more the soaring eagle, we can once again perceive a national pride in our ability to perform like a well-coordinated team. Now is the time to wake-up. We can begin to negotiate with leverage and begin to compete as a team, joining in competition with leverage at our disposal. Competition is better than anger or war; and its resultant progress in science, technology and art are far more enjoyable.

## VALUE #6: CAPITAL—Indebtedness vs. Solvency

*By exercising restraint, buying functional products not fads, buyers can increase one another's profits and wages. When these are invested in creative new enterprises or saving accounts they result in cycles of growth and new accumulations of wealth, without having to sell assets to overseas investors.*

What is wrong with our attitude about indebtedness and how can we change it to strengthen our Nation?

We became complacent about assuming indebtedness, both personal indebtedness and governmental indebtedness, in order to have continued prosperity. It's self-indulgent to buy prosperity today, asking our children to pay for it tomorrow.

We are the ones who elect Presidents, Senators and Congressmen campaigning on a platform of "no new taxes but vast new increases in expenditures for armaments, hazardous waste cleanups, bank bailouts, prison construction, etc., etc." There never was any secret about how that was to be done, nor was it by magic.

In the 1980's everyone knew the "years of prosperity" were based on spending money we didn't have. We borrowed from the newly wealthy Nations of the world. Everyone talked openly about national deficits, negative balance of trade payments and devaluation of the dollar. Americans consciously chose to indulge themselves both by selling inherited assets and by borrowing against the future payback capability of our children. That was a clear violation of the trust given us by prior generations and a crime against our own children.

The prevalent feeling amongst Americans was one of satiating all the appetites they could afford, or get credit to afford. America's vision paradigm since the 1970's has been an assumption that since there was only one life to live, let's live life to its fullest by satiating ourselves with as many "things" we can purchase in life.

The self-indulgent conclusion to this vision paradigm was that more "things" were desired. This made Americans act like the spoiled children in the movie "Willie Wonka and the Chocolate Factory." They were saying to themselves "I want it NOW!" so they competed with one another intensely to get "the good life," showing it off to Mr. Jones who was trying to keep up.

During the 1980's our National debt skyrocketed. We exported our liquid capital by two principle types of purchases. First by purchasing "perishable" goods and services from overseas companies. Second by choosing to defend the world against communism without requiring other prosperous Democratic Nations to contribute capital or technology.

In the first purchase we received perishable consumer goods in return for our money. In the second purchase we purchased perishable military hardware such as MX missiles, B2 bombers, Abrams tanks, Osprey fighter planes and Star Wars. These costs could have and should have been shared with other Nations who wanted to remain free of communism or we should have abstained from such frivolous expenditures.

The exporting of liquid capital resulted! Newly rich overseas entrepreneurs rapidly reinvested their wealth in the purchase of a "non-perishable" piece of America. Whether land, buildings, corporations, stocks, bonds, farms, mines or golf resorts; their investments were wise whereas ours were foolish.

Tariffs, trade barriers or other governmental legislation to prohibit ownership of business and/or land in America is not, and never will be, a solution for controlling the interests of overseas investors. The best way to achieve control is to voluntarily commit to recycling the wealth of our Nation by buying American products and services. The denial of capital to overseas products and the reinvestment of capital in R and D for new technology will encourage domestic growth and prosperity.

*Visualize a new American attitude* in which investment capital, coming from either profits by American owners or savings by American laborers, working together to encourage focused teams. Either form of capital encourages growth by American owned companies and denies growth to overseas investors. What is more it makes capital available at lower interest rates than would be available from overseas investors and retains banking profits in America, instead of being exported to overseas banks.

Of particular value to a growing economy are growing industries, in which the profits generated are reinvested directly into the business. Whether the profits are used for expansion of plant, upgrading of equipment, research or development of related products; it's the single most effective way to utilize capital. Reinvesting capital in an existing or related business is the perfect mix, because the expertise of the company's management and staff give the greatest control over expenditures being made. Control of resources—including labor, materials, equipment supplies, capital and time (there are no other resources)—can best be accomplished by people who know the business well.

Failure frequently occurs when capital is used in take-over attempts by moneyed investors who know little of the business, or even when profits are reinvested in diversified industries having no relation to the primary industry generating profits. Whenever capital is obtained by borrowing or by issuing shares, the provider of capital is not in close control of its use.

Hence the motivation to use investment capital, borrowed or one's own, should be thought of as most effective when investing in one's own business or the corporation at which one works. If investing is like gambling on a horserace, it's best to place your bet on your own nose or that of someone you know and respect.

Lack of knowledge was a major reason why the feeding frenzy of junk bond take-over attempts was destined to fail. The corporate raiders always blamed management for being inept at protecting shareholder interests (i.e., not maximizing their quarterly return on investment). But management perceived the raiders would not only fire them and their employees, but would also try to sell-off the companies assets since they did not have any idea about how to run the company on a long-term basis. Both were right in their parochial viewpoints, but diametrically opposed to America's best interests of long-term investing for creation and innovation of new industries as well as new jobs.

To create new wealth, all Americans have a role. One of our greatest weaknesses is spending to our limit of credit, minimizing savings. Credit buying is not wrong; its just too many people have taken it to excess by living beyond the edge of their income, without any balance between savings and indebtedness.

Today's depleted savings leave far less money available for investment. With the need for more investment in R&D, a domestic source of money can only be obtained if Americans limit spending, particularly for durable goods from overseas. The money spent on such perishable items drains enormous sums of capital from the economy. This leaves overseas banks and investors as a primary source of capital for entrepreneurs, innovators, corporations and even Government agencies. In the private sector these loans frequently involve selling-off an equity position in the new venture, which the overseas investor does not fear because his assets are out of reach for American courts. And the downhill spiral continues!

Americans need to begin saving instead of borrowing to the limit. We can still lead the "good life," albeit with limitations. Economic austerity and conservation of natural resources for the next several years, by voluntarily refraining from buying or at least limiting the frequency of buying overseas products, will go a long way towards revitalizing America. The impact of savings on the economy will be dramatic if each American family does its part, pumping its savings into economic recovery and growth, either by direct investment or by pooling capital in investment funds or banks.

Direct investment of time, money and effort is best. Simply investing money in stocks, bonds, real estate or gold mines is similar to betting on horses or rolling dice. It requires a bit more research but in the end luck is the determining factor for investment success. Direct investment in one's own entrepreneurial business, on the other hand, requires creativity, determination, perseverance, time and effort. Contributions to society, economic recovery and growth are magnified when personal effort (perhaps even family effort) and capital are expended over a period of time.

We can be concerned about the purchase of land and businesses by overseas interests? But concern stems from one criterion and one criterion only. Is the overseas interest committed to the best interests of America or of some other Nation? If the answer to that question is America, the next question is obvious. Are they willing to become a citizen of the United States and pledge allegiance to it *and no other country*?

Educated persons and wealthy persons wishing to come to America and become valued citizens, can be made welcome. Emma Lazarus wrote on the foundation stone of the Statue of Liberty, "Give Us Your Tired, Your Poor and Your Hungry," and the tired, poor and hungry people of Europe responded by building the melting pot of freedom and creativity called America. But where is it written that only the tired, poor and hungry are welcome?

America has and can always welcome the educated, rich and well-fed of the world who desire to come here and establish a life of freedom and creativity. America offers not only Democracy, freedom and creative opportunity to such people; it also offers political stability not available in many other Nations.

## VALUE #7: REWARDS & ACCLAIM—Entertainers vs. Innovators

*By rethinking how buyers reward and acclaim those who compete successfully and contribute most to our society, buyers can incite innovation. Establishing competitions could make mental prowess more rewarding than physical prowess or entertaining good looks.*

What is wrong with our attitude about the distribution of wealth in America and how can we change it to strengthen our Nation?

Our weakness is we value goods and services in a distorted manner, with entertainment earning our highest spending priority. Our heroes are actresses and quarterbacks, with our highest paying reward system going to those who entertain us.

Entertainment is Americana at its best, but its rewards have gotten out of proportion with other vocations that contribute to prosperity. With the advent of television, income from sporting events spread beyond gate receipts from fans at the ballpark to all people who buy advertised products, such as beer and cars. Hence even those not interested in a boxing match get to pay the purse.

A shift in attitude, awarding public acclaim and monetary rewards to those who create new ideas and develop new jobs, enabling *all Americans* to compete for such acclaim and rewards. The incentive to create a mental competition, rather than one based on facial appearance or physical attributes would become universal instead of being limited to the few who are physically gifted. Children would readily perceive opportunities afforded by this competition and strive for education and creativity. Hopefully adolescents would move away from the hopelessness and despair that is a basis of today's apathy.

*Visualize a new American attitude* in which Americans acclaim and reward those who innovate new solutions to society's problems, so all are encouraged to compete for major breakthroughs. Both Government, corporations and persons of wealth can use their resources to sponsor competitions, thereby spreading monetary rewards and acclaim throughout society. Certainly a voluntary and direct redistribution of wealth, to adults and adolescents who strive to attain innovative solutions in numerous competitions, will be a far more effective use of money than frivolous buying.

Numerous competitions could be held having sufficient monetary rewards to motivate adults and adolescents to strive for excellence as a means of supplementing their family's income. Monetary awards and acclaim are primary motivators. In wealthier neighborhoods monetary awards would enable children to compete and earn their own money and self-respect. Children would be able to recognize attainable objectives, making education their hope for an improved lifestyle and ending both the drug cultures and other cult cultures of despair.

In industry, competitions can be established within the work force to encourage solution of society's most pressing problems. Rewards and acclaim may not be made for several years as competitors strive for excellence in attaining the goal, either as individuals within companies or as private persons. Acclaim can be focused on individuals of successful teams, not just the team itself.

Innovators can be encouraged to probe the realm of what is possible, even though it doesn't seem probable. Society, through its legislators can establish broad policy objectives. The buying public would thereby set the goals and establish rewards available to all members of society. It might not be too surprising if most awards go to individual entrepreneurs and even young students, having limited resources. Ingenuity and creativity will leap out from every direction if society is receptive to it and aggressively encourages progress.

By consciously and intensively focusing our Nation's system of rewarding and acclaiming its citizens, we can establish a mental focus and direct people's energy in directions society thinks best. Each of us perceived the

"American Dream" in our youth, only to find out reality was not as perfect as we had imagined. We can make that dream a reality for future Americans.

Suppose in restructuring rewards and acclaim we not only set up competitions but also established an individual, one-on-one sponsorship program for each youth. The sponsorship of adolescents, with parental approval for youths and graduates entering the work force, would provide each with a level of confidence focused on achieving. The sponsor can be personally supportive, taking a direct interest both in guiding and in training for career objectives.

If the youth is musically inclined or technically inclined, an appropriate sponsor can volunteer. Should the sponsor be able to provide financial support as a patron, monetary support can be acceptable within well-defined limits but not encouraged. The primary objective being to give of one's time and knowledge, nurturing youths into being "all they can be." Children yearn for intensive one-on-one eye contact with adults, whether parent or teacher or sponsor.

America's future can be a brilliant light for the world to see, if our youth can leave disenchantment behind and realize the American dream is an ever-improving reality. A reality in which each generation of youth is counseled by their proceeding generations in a nurturing environment, recognizing the importance of continuity and the joy of sharing will attain goals far beyond our imagining.

# VALUE #8: PLANNING—Quick Profits vs. Long Range Plans

*By focusing on a Common Vision for long-range planning and invest-ment both in the private sector and public sector, more monies could be invested in research and development of new products and better plant facilities, instead of just maximizing quarterly returns on investment.*

What is wrong with our attitude about planning in America and how can we change it to strengthen our Nation?

Our weakness is the manner in which we make decisions and measure performance. It's an attitude within our society dictating a short-term focus, based on human greed. "What's in it for me now? " or "What is the short-term (quarterly) return on investment? " becomes the rationale, rather than the long-term impact of "What will this decision mean ten years from now to me, to my children, to my company, to my country? "

Consider an American executive who currently wants to invest in a long-range plan. The executive comes to the office Monday morning and finds the culmination of a year-long, $20 million research and develop-ment (R&D) project sitting on the desk. On operating this first proto-type, it works perfectly. Surely it will fulfill the needs of the multimillion-dollar market for which it was designed.

But now our executive must decide whether to propose to the Board of Directors they invest an additional $100 million to build a plant, buy equipment, hire and train people, obtain environmental permits, adver-tise, etc. or sell all rights to an overseas manufacturer for $40 million, thereby providing an immediate profit of $20 million and a 100 percent return-on-investment in one year. American managers are trained to take this latter alternative.

If our executive were to fight for domestic manufacture and worldwide marketing, a shareholder revolt would in all likelihood result. It would be led by a corporate raider such as Pickens, Icahn or Lorenzo, challenging the exec-utive for having dared not to maximize last quarter's return to the investors.

An scenario, following an unlikely decision by our executive to manufacture the new product, would present management with the option of building the new manufacturing facility in the U. S. or overseas. A decision to build overseas would in all likelihood result, based on:

o Lower wage scales and overhead for a captive overseas work force,

o Lesser costs due to an absence of environmental restraints,

o Less exposure to liability from product users, employees or class-action lawsuits,

o Availability of overseas funding, and

o Availability of "free" overseas land, with little consideration given to the impact on America or the exodus of jobs.

So even where research results in a new product, American managers are trained and pressured to maximize an immediate return on investment by selling technology to overseas manufacturers, manufacturing in an overseas subsidiary or contracting the manufacturing to a private overseas company. Our MBA programs teach this as the right thing to do in the best interest of the shareholders. To do otherwise would again be vulnerable to a shareholder revolt or take-over bid from some get-rich-quick schemer who wants a fast sell-off of assets.

The basis of the shareholder revolt would be loss of profits from sale of the technology and the high expenses being incurred, either by reinvesting profit instead of paying dividends or by incurring debt. This attitude is the business equivalent of rape, quickly stripping a company of its fixed assets in order to attain liquidity and maximize short-term shareholder returns. Foregoing far greater long-term potential is an injustice to both the company, its employees and America.

Government and its elected officials also think in terms of short-term "quick fixes." Our politicians assume that if Government tinkers with the right buttons, all ills will vanish. The ills never vanish because tinkering with interest rates, tax rate changes, borrowing limits, balanced budgets, spending limits, lower wage scales or other economic controls can not correct the real problem. Important as all these are, they remain short-term expedient corrections, not "a solution" to the more deeply rooted long-term problems facing our Nation. These problems are deeply rooted in American's psyche and go far beyond Government spending to individual and corporate spending habits throughout our economy.

*Visualize a new American attitude* in which Americans insist elected officials, union officials and business executives shift planning away from short-term fixes, to focus on long-term solutions. Planning at all levels of Government, business and labor would evolve from well thought through programs. Each program focusing on attaining higher levels of employment in our labor force at much higher living standards.

Buyer loyalty to American products deserves executive loyalty to American jobs. Executive loyalty, caring for the jobs of fellow Americans will avoid the costly drain of having to care for family's welfare after jobs are lost. An absence of planning has caused many of our manufacturing jobs to be exported overseas, reducing salary levels, reducing employment and increasing social costs for unemployment and prisons. These drains on our economy result in a loss of economic vitality as costs go up to pay for sorely needed social requirements, a vicious cycle of decline.

A new attitude of loyalty, focused on a coordinated program between Government, the private business sector, public interest groups and organized labor can reorient our planning priorities, as needed to create new technologies and new industries. The competitive attitude of striving is best done by a coordinated team, with high levels of trust in one another. Government, business, management and labor can recognize and agree on certain objectives, seeking to bring individual ingenuity to the fore so new industries are created.

The primary source of strength available to break America's downhill slide is American buyers and their power-of-the-purse. If people commit in advance to buying products of value created by our innovators, the downhill spiral can be turned around. The power-of-the-purse has always been there. We just haven't recognized its value.

Long-range planning can be focused on new products having the most likelihood of success in the new market. New American industries will spring up rapidly as innovators and investors respond to new markets, in an atmosphere of trust. Trust that most citizens can be counted on to "Buy American" for the Nation's well being. Yankee ingenuity will make major breakthroughs in new consumer products, however consumers should demand all such products be environmentally sound, with prices including closed-system recycling of waste streams.

# VALUE #9: LITIGATION—Greedy Adversaries vs. Trust Between Competitors

*By stopping the litigious drain on society, investors could again take calculated risks in which only invested capital is at risk. Today investors put all assets at risk on innovative products that could in any way harm someone. Limits of liability can be established for innovative products. Americans can stop suing and begin trusting one another.*

What is wrong with our attitude about litigation in America and how can we change it to strengthen our Nation?

Our weakness is the frequency and ease with which we sue one another for exorbitant sums. This is not the fault of lawyers so let's not point the finger at them. Instead point the finger at ourselves, American society as a whole. Our habit of suing one another stems from basic human greed and a desire to get rich quick. Lawyers only help greedy people get greedier.

The impact of our litigious society is devastating to the economy. Only secondarily is it devastating in the non-productive nature of legal action. Its primary negative impact is the manner in which it prevents creativity and innovation. The risk of being sued for an innovative product prevents American investors from competing with overseas companies because they are too likely to be sued for all their assets. Why should wealthy people invest in a new product when total success will only make them very rich and partial success, not to mention failure, can lead to endless litigation and poverty?

It's not the risk of investing capital that stops investment in new technology. Rather, it's the risk of all the investor's assets should lawsuits result. Sometimes spurious lawsuits result even when new technology does work as planned. Hence only overseas investors, with assets largely out of reach of American courts, can afford to take such risks. Domestic companies can not price such enormous risks into their product costs and still compete.

Bringing capital and new technology together is frequently impossible in America today because of concerns about liability. If, the new technology has some risk potential, such as ingested medicines or products which could later be found to release carcinogens, this leaves the investor and the innovator vulnerable to lawsuits. Legal challenges not only cause lost profits but also seek enormous punitive damages. Large judgements awarded during past years put all the investor's assets at risk on every investment. Little wonder American investment is focused on low-risk projects like computer software, real estate and entertainment.

In contrast, the attitude of Japanese society is to entirely reject the concept of suing one another. That permits their society to innovate freely both here and at home. During two trips the authors made to Japan a few years ago, a first hand experience demonstrated the intensity with which the Japanese discourage lawsuits.

In the Japan Times there was a story, reported on page 1, about two families struck by tragedy. The mothers of both families were good friends who frequently cared for one another's children. Sadly, one mother came home from shopping one day to find her child had wandered off unobserved by the babysitting mother and had drowned in a nearby drainage channel. The grieving family thereupon sued the other family, which is a virtually unheard of action in Japan. Hence its merit as a page 1 story.

On returning to Japan a month later it was surprising to find this same story was still headline news. During that month the phone hadn't stopped ringing at the grieving family's home, as indignant and angry people from across the Nation called to chastise them for taking legal action. The grieving father lost his lifetime employment because of the legal action and newspapers throughout the country criticized he and his wife intensely. They were often chastised for trying to hurt Japan by making it like America. After one month the grieving family withdrew its lawsuit due to the intense peer pressure brought on it by society.

That is the nature of one of our competitors. Their entire society is intolerant of litigation and does not hesitate to bring intense peer pressure to bear when individuals disrupt their society's mores. To some Americans this may appear to be tyranny of the majority, but to the Japanese it is society's best interest that comes first.

*Visualize a new American attitude* in which Americans pledge to stop suing one another for sums far exceeding actual losses. Legislation could limit such lawsuits, but that can only be a second line of defense. Of far more importance is societal pressure, such as a friend showing annoyance to another friend for a frivolous lawsuit, instead of winking and saying good luck. Peer pressure is very powerful.

Legislation could be passed to effectively limit damages to actual loses, including suffering but excluding punitive damages and loss of enjoyment. Only gross negligence or criminal action should be subject to punitive damages and unlimited liability.

Plaintiffs could also be made responsible for all defendant legal costs if the suit is lost, so those spurious suits will stop. Spurious litigation destroys trust relationships, which can be the cornerstone of interpersonal relations throughout America, particularly in business. Without an attitude of trust and the freedom to innovate, America's decline will continue.

New technological innovation thought to have a low-risk potential, can be granted hold-harmless status making inventors and investors immune to lawsuit. Even where the risk potential is too high to consider hold-harmless status, a limit of liability can be established so insurance can be purchased. This will permit pricing of the product so it can reflect appropriate insurance premiums. An infinite risk is not insurable, but a limit of liability makes the risk calculable for insurance rating.

Conflict relationships such as shareholders vs. management, management vs. labor, management vs. public interest groups, etc. can be diffused in the absence of litigation. Fresh understandings and open communications can be brought to bear, making decisions that factor in a vantage point of what is best in the long-term interest of the Nation. Continuity of operations need not be disrupted by disputes. All sides can strive to attain prosperity for one another, with an equitable sharing of profits and wages.

When differences of opinion prevent a consensus, the solution can not be resolved by take-over attempts, class action lawsuits or strikes. The solution can instead be reached through negotiation, voting and peer pressure seeking to advance progress and consensus. The use of mediators can be encouraged, wherein informal out-of-court settlements are reached. If mediation fails then private judging, by a retired judge, can be attempted so matters can be resolved out-of-court. Both these methods tend to drive home the win-win nature of settling disputes before everybody loses. That is the nature of litigation, wherein the real costs are always far greater than the final settlement.

## VALUE #10: PEER PRESSURE—Individual Excess vs. Society's Restraints

*By exerting peer pressure on one another, Americans can cause conformity without uniformity. Peer pressure is far more flexible and timely than writing new legislation and using police powers to enforce it. Legal action through Government is not as effective as pride earned with family and friends in the community.*

What is wrong with our attitudes for restraining individuals who violate our customs and mores, and how can we change it to strengthen our Nation?

The American people have lost something of value during the past few decades. We lost the strength and Common Vision that comes from a society's "collective values. " These collective values are especially valuable under a free enterprise system with a Democratic form of Government. It provides a totally flexible way in which good people can rapidly control people of ill will, without having to ask Government to intervene on their behalf.

Our knee-jerk reaction during the past decades has been to ask Government to legislate away all of society's ills. It is far more effective to do it ourselves through peer pressure, without vigilantes or guns. Legislative action occurs after the fact and depends on police power. It's a fall-back position for a society whose people are too complacent to take direct action. Frequently legislative action and police power are too little, too late to do any good. Peer pressure is far more effective!

People who believe strongly about an issue, no matter how emotional it is, can apply peer pressure. Whether it be abortion rights, flag burning, buying American products, suing for frivolous injury, voter apathy, etc., peer pressure is far more effective than legislation and police power. Friend-to-friend encouragement is the best kind of positive peer pressure but ostracism is a form of negative peer pressure available at the spectrum's opposite end.

Peer pressure can extend to the media as well. For example if enough people let the media know they do not consider flag burning a media event or interviews with terrorists to be appropriate news information, both flag burning and terrorism would reduce drastically. Both are staged events designed to focus our attention on their parochial message. Hence it's the public, not the media, needing to act. If people cared enough to let the media know they would boycott those media stations and advertisers who gave access to flag burners and terrorists, such coverage would stop overnight. There would be no need to escalate to legal action or police action, thereby giving even more publicity to obnoxious positions on the streets and in the courts.

Because we are such an individualistic society in America, we lost certain advantages competitor Nations have. The individual rights guaranteed by the Bill of Rights, 225 years ago, have been legally interpreted to emphasize the rights of individuals when they come in conflict with society's perceived best interests.

*Visualize a new American attitude* in which a group of people within our society, having collective values and common ideals maintained through direct contact, effectively exert peer pressure on one another. If they choose to exert pressures on other people or counter a group committed to opposite ideals, it's right and proper for them to demonstrate their ideals as vocally as they wish, within non-violent legal bounds.

Americans have become inured to the excesses of certain individuals in society. Excesses are frequently met with apathy and complacency rather than outrage. Where outrage could have been expressed when Fujitsu sold America's secret submarine ball bearing technology to Russia, thereby voiding our ability to detect Russian submarine's locations, there was hardly a voice raised in protest seeking a boycott at the cash register against Fujitsu's imported products.

Americans rarely chastise tax evaders and inside traders. This results in a clear message to immoral people that everything short of illegal activity will be tolerated and even winked at approvingly if they can get away with it. We even go so far as saying if caught at white-collar crime, penalties will be slight and perhaps even worthwhile.

Visualize instead an attitude in which people take action against violators of established norms. The action need only be peer pressure, frowning on minor transgressions and ostracizing people who make major transgressions. This kind of social pressure works far better than any legal action by police or the courts.

Consider the pressure brought on the Japanese couple who sued their neighbors over the drowning of their child. That kind of outrage by an entire society and its press, curbed what it considered an excessive "Americanization" of their legal system. What we have come to accept as proper, they abhor. What they have come to accept as proper peer pressure, we abhor as a tyranny of the majority.

Peer pressure, if exerted properly, would result in far less legal action and far more honesty in personal relations between people. If ones word were ones bond and a bad reputation in the community meant something negative, people would conform to honesty norms voluntarily. If peer pressure were exerted properly, such conformance would not limit innovation or cause a tyranny of the majority.

The wide use of peer pressure; by simply frowning at a friend's unethical behavior, scolding a friend for immoral behavior or informing the law for illegal behavior, would encourage individual judgement about normal behavior patterns. Uniformity of behavior would not be regarded as a straight-jacket on individualism and innovation; rather it can be regarded as a leveling of the playing field. This would permit individuals to compete without giving people of ill-will a head-start advantage.

Clearly when it comes to encouraging friends and neighbors to buy American products, peer pressure is the best way to encourage conformance. To try to legislate a Buy American program or cause it to happen by raising tariff barriers would be foolish. However a voluntary grass roots program, subscribed to by a vast number of vocal Americans would rapidly turn the tide.

Visualize the impact on our economy if the neighbor who buys an imported status symbol car, camera or suit of clothes suddenly found the purchase earned scorn and ridicule on the part of neighbors and friends instead of awe and respect. It would soon become apparent to all peers that loyalty to American products is regarded of paramount importance and violation of loyalty would earn disrespect every time.

Similarly visualize a now common scenario in which someone mentions filing a lawsuit over a trivial matter or for punitive damages far exceeding the loss incurred. If the friend chastises the litigant for abusing the legal system and being disloyal to the best interests of America, such spurious litigation would be severely curtailed.

Peer pressure would also be of great value in countering apathy. Whether its voter apathy or apathy about someone losing a job, being chastised by a friend is the best cure for not letting it happen again.

As another example of exerting peer pressure, consider the highly charged actions on pro-choice and anti-abortion forces. Each has exerted peer pressure very appropriately both before the media and in direct confrontation, whenever they chose to do so without violence. Violence is never excusable! Legislative action and police force should enforce non-violence and disruption to the fullest extent of the law. It's far more effective to demonstrate in the streets in vehement confrontation.

People who have an enclave of friends believing strongly about an issue, will likely engage in dialogue and have pressure brought to bear on that issue. That type of dialogue is desirable unless the individual chooses to make a new set of friends, say by joining another club. Intense communications between people can be encouraged, not just on national issues but the smaller issues impacting our daily lives as well.

These examples demonstrate the very positive nature of peer pressure once it becomes a prevalent attitude. Today the prevalent attitude is indifference and complacency, which encourages people to disregard societal needs as they focus only on self-interest.

## VALUE #11: DEMOCRACY—Corruption vs. Freedom

*By evolving our Democracy, America can become a more responsive society, in which both individual freedom is maximized and individual control over society is maximized. In order to level the playing field in every election, only taxpayer funds should be spent on campaigns up to a pre-established limit for each office. No candidate would have a monetary advantage at the outset of any campaign and no one is beholden to wealthy contributors for gifts. Any such gifts to an elected official should result in long prison terms for both the politician and the donor.*

What is wrong with our attitude towards Democracy and how can we change it to strengthen our Nation?

Certainly there has been no form of government in the history of mankind more deserving of people's trust than Jeffersonian Democracy. Recent events in Russia and the clamoring for freedom in the world is an enormous compliment to Jefferson and America's Founding Fathers over 225-years ago.

Democracy evolved only recently! In 1776 it was inscribed in the Declaration of Independence and Constitution as America's *first great step* in the revolt of all common peoples' (i.e., not royalty) against millennia of tyranny. Tyrannical kings and sultans were unquestioned absolute dictators, ruling by accident of birth. For over 4,500-years the entire world was ruled by absolute dictators, having various titles and names recorded in a history written under their tight control. Most all of royalty was oppressive and brutal landowners! A few were just oppressive, so history refers to them as "benevolent" royalty.

Hence prior to Democracy being established in America, people throughout the world lived under the tyranny and whim of dictators. Even vastly heralded documents of history, such as the Magna Carta, did little more than delegate tyranny over the people of England to another level of tyrants. It enabled tyranny to be managed at the local level by despotic nobles who reported back to the king for final decision-making.

Although history has shown dictatorships can usually take action faster than Democracies, it also shows they make mistakes having a very high price for the vast majority of people. Between suffering through the drudgery of heavy low-paying work and the torture of vicious wars, the difficulties in common peoples' lives were of little concern to royalty or nobility.

Even though Democracy is always better than dictatorship, Democracy can still be corrupted. A corrupt Democracy serves as a political curtain, behind which power is usurped in varying degrees, such as:

Degree I:    Ballot box stuffing wherein a politician uses Democracy as a cloak for election to office.

Degree II:   Corrupt politicians who sell influence and votes to wealthy persons.

Degree III:  Political pressure that uses duress to influence the outcome of a vote.

Degree IV:   Political manipulation that uses lies to influence the outcome of a vote.

Degree V:    Political deceit that uses false image-making instead of substantive issues to influence the outcome of a vote.

*Visualize a new American attitude* in which the vast majority of people are assumed to have honest and ethical values, even though each also have very natural self-serving interests. Good will and ethical values are the strength of our Democracy. The will of people to trust one another in a Democracy is the only shield against tyranny. To sustain that trust, powerful interest groups have to be permitted to form and lobby, but not with excessive power.

Democracy is the buffer to avoid such excesses. Democracy provides people with an opportunity to control their collective destiny. That is not to say Democracy is immune to error on certain issues affecting peoples' well-being. People do make mistakes when voting. But where people are free to vote their collective conscience, those mistakes are random and occasional. This protects against long-term corruption of values.

The American experiment, and an experiment it still is, is still in its infancy. To say no suffrage existed during all those millennia before 1776 is to say freedom is newborn at 225-years old and still evolving. Women had never voted or owned property until only 80-years ago. Blacks and Hispanics could not truly vote until 30-years ago. Change is rampant!

There is no reason for us to think of Democracy as stagnant. Rather it is ripe for New Ideas and New Ideals of freedom. If both freedom and Democracy in America are still in their infancy, they need to be nurtured and strengthened. Both are still clearly flawed by corruption and self-serving groups having too much power.

The elimination of corruption and influence has been a constant struggle in America during the past 225-years. Certainly we've reached a level of comfort with our Government as reflective of the will of the people. However that is not a reason to be complacent or stop the evolution of freedom. Freedom can only be had by continually making Democracy better reflect the will of people. Decisions made collectively, based on random voting by numerous individuals, are always more reliable than decisions made by a small group of wealthy politicians and lobbyists or by absolute dictators and kings.

Hence continuing the evolution of both Democracy and freedom can be an on-going effort. New Ideas and New Ideals can be under constant evaluation and scrutiny, determining the best way to make Democracy better reflect the will of the people.

The will of the people gets back to the concept of a level playing field for competition in all walks of life. Democracy affords us the freedom and liberty to structure our society as we see fit, so the wealthy person does not have more power than the poor person and voter apathy is turned into voter enthusiasm. These are the two most important changes needed in American Democracy at this time.

The current process of electing representatives for city, county, state or federal offices; purposefully makes representatives directly dependent on wealthy people to pay the high cost of election campaigning. In order to level the playing field in every election, only taxpayer funds would be spent on campaigns up to a pre-established limit for each office. As in a game of Monopoly, no candidate would have a monetary advantage at the outset of any campaign and no one is beholden to wealthy contributors for gifts. Any such gifts to an elected official should result in long prison terms for both the politician and the donor.

If all candidates for election had the same limit on spending, as provided them from taxpayer coffers, all elected officials would be beholden only to the electorate. Expensive image-making commercials would no longer be the focus of expensive campaigns, leading to voter apathy. Instead issues confronting the electorate would become the focus of in-depth information and hotly contested debates.

Because most Americans have good, honest and ethical values, they can trust their own judgement about changing the nature of their Democracy. As long as the changes move towards greater pluralism and statistical diversity, wherein there is less likelihood for power and control being concentrated within small groups of individuals, change can be encouraged.

# VALUE #12: VOTING—Apathy vs. Enhancing Democracy

*By giving Americans the right to vote on issues too close to call in the Congress, State or local Legislatures, representative government can be enhanced. By dialing an 800 number and voting on well-publicized issues, voter apathy will disappear and decisions will better reflect the majority's desires.*

What is wrong with our attitude about voting in America and how can we change it to strengthen our Nation?

Americans seem to view Government with suspicion. Many treat it with disrespect because they suspect influence peddling at best and outright corruption at worst, is prevalent. This attitude, assuming powerful and wealthy people have already purchased the political system, causes apathy at the voting booth and also throughout American society.

Americans simply do not recognize their collective power. They don't realize they control the purse strings at the cash register and votes at the polls, giving them enormous power and a leading role to play in how technology evolves. When Americans spoke up clearly and said they wanted a cure for polio or heart disease or they wanted hazardous wastes cleaned up or go to the moon; the political system delivered on those efforts. Today we are letting technology evolve without first having American society set broad policy guidelines.

That is not to say total success will always be achieved. But only the electorate can effectively take the leadership role in setting policy to prioritize R&D funding. This is far better than leaving decision-making to politicians or technicians who happen to have the wealth and political clout to get a self-serving program passed by Congress and the President. Public initiative, based on divergent expert information, is sorely needed in setting priorities.

*Visualize a new American attitude* in which Americans recognize it takes bravery and courage to make decisions and to see them through to fruition. Decisions made by society can be supported by all of the people, once the majority decides them. People who advocate a minority opinion can get enthusiastically behind efforts to make the majority decision work effectively for them.

If society, through the will of the majority, learns to set priorities for the monetary resources at its disposal by asking that specific things be accomplished; they will be. As Bobby Kennedy phrased it, "Some people ask why, I ask why not."

Historically, true Democratic government was lost when Town Hall meetings were abandoned in favor of representative government. A representative form of government was necessitated by the unwieldy size of the populace, as towns grew into cities and cities combined into states. Representative government was, and still is, the only logical alternative to anarchy and dictatorship.

But American history for the past two centuries shows many pitfalls in the operation of our representative government. When an apathetic electorate permits individuals to assume excessive power, these individuals will frequently become corrupt or have already been corrupted. This corruption has proven an enormous drain on society. Yet it has been allowed to continue for extended periods of time.

Apathy was unavoidable until now. Involving people in the direct solution of issues by returning to a Town Hall form of government, with millions of participants, was a physically impossibility. But it no longer is! Voting on issues is now possible and is, in fact, becoming more practical with each passing year as communication technology blossoms into more sophisticated applications.

To actually return to the Town Hall, where each citizen of America has an opportunity to speak, is not necessary. It is however within the realm of present day technology to open up the legislative process to direct public opinion. In so doing, the electorate would become more involved in the decision-making process, rather than merely in the process of electing a representative. The current process of electing representatives for city, county, state or federal offices; purposefully makes representatives directly dependent on wealthy people to pay the high cost of election campaigning.

One way to increase involvement, within the framework of our existing system of representative government, would be for *each* legislative body to call for a plebiscite on *all* issues not resolved nay or yea, with a 52 percent majority.

Representatives would then be more directly responsive to popular support of the majority interests. Where the issue is clear-cut and the will of the elected representatives exceeds the 52 percent limit, there is no need to involve the electorate. But when the vote is so close as to indicate indecision about the correct course of action, only the electorate should control the outcome.

This could be accomplished in monthly elections, the ballot for which would consist of all such issues on a national, state and local basis. Using electronic balloting, the counting could be accomplished quickly and economically, with people voting by telephone in the privacy of their homes. To bring our representative Democracy back to its origins, the electronic age can use television, radio talk shows, the internet and "800" telephone numbers.

Consider a crucial issue not getting a two-vote margin in the Senate or a five-vote margin in the House. That's too close to call! So let the people decide by an election plebiscite. For two weeks let television, radio, internet chat rooms, magazines and newspapers present debates about the issue, with experts and lay people arguing pro and con.

Then let an informed electorate decide the issue by dialing an "800" number, followed by a social security number and secret "Personal Identification Number (PIN)" number. Once authorized, the voter can cast a simple yes or a no vote, or even a choice amongst a few alternatives. Imagine the impact voting on issues would have on Americans. Skepticism and apathy would disappear overnight and political influence peddling would be drastically reduced.

In this manner all voters would have a direct and continual influence on the course of action Government takes at all levels. The apathy prevalent today would dissolve to a great extent as the electorate recognized its increased responsibility and timely participation in America's decision-making. Our existing media of mass communications can readily fulfill demand for information on which to make decisions. Legislators most deeply involved in each vote could appear on television to present the pros and cons of each issue during the week prior to Election Day. Newspapers, television and libraries would remain as primary resources of detailed information.

By direct involvement of an enlightened electorate, Government could be made a more responsive servant of society. With apathy banished, people could make policy decisions on a more frequent basis. In the technical arena we could initiate breakthroughs of vast proportion simply by asking for it. Who ever thought Mankind would actually walk on the Moon when President Kennedy announced it in 1962?

Why does society accept a status quo and not demand better solutions? Because society is fatalistic and assumes if someone else isn't doing something, then it most likely can't be done. It's just such fatalistic attitudes in need of change. Only then can people firmly believe in what was proven by the numerous scientific advances made during the 20th Century; "the impossible only takes a little longer."

We can all take that same attitude if we are to improve the world we live in by proactive thought and control, instead of reactive knee-jerk reflexes. For example, it's not enough to react with billion dollar programs to remove hazardous wastes at 40-year old toxic disposal sites or to spend $100 billion to clean-up an earthquake ravaged city which could have been spared the disaster by spending $100 million.

Proactive thought control can tell taxpayers that toxic dumping is wrong and the costs of proper disposal is much less expensive, and far safer, than toxic dump clean-up. Similarly, common sense tells us it's more cost-effective to spend millions to totally prevent earthquake damage to buildings and loss of life, than to spend billions repairing devastated cities after an earthquake has wrecked its havoc.

## VALUE #13: POLITICAL ACTION—Tilted Playing Field vs. Fair Competition

*By maintaining a level playing field for all aspects of domestic and international competition, Americans can again grow and prosper without debt or unbalanced exports. Self-imposed economic handicaps can be removed, perhaps by political action for specific legislation.*

What is wrong with our attitude in choosing political direction and how can we change it to strengthen our Nation?

Political leadership of the past few decades was clearly chosen by the American people with a mandate to spend and to borrow. The issues were clearly defined and the vote was decisive. We consciously chose prosperity and defense spending, unpaid at minimal tax rates and knowing the burden of our spending spree would have to be paid later by our children. What an inheritance! We must be the first American generation to leave its children a negative inheritance, without any wars to excuse it.

Americans alone in the world aggressively seek to buy overseas products in preference to domestic products. That is a drain on our well-being other Nations do not contend with. America has also withstood alone the costly burden of a military standoff with totalitarianism for too many years. That too is a drain other Nations do not contend with.

Hence if America acts to recapture what it has so casually given away, its economic well-being, it will be leveling what has been a tilted playing field. The handicap given to America's trading partners in years past is simply being withdrawn.

For one trading partner to have removed all economic barriers unilaterally, as America did, without having comparable access to other Nation's markets was altruistic. We have paid the price for our altruism and can now halt that practice. Allegiance to persons closest to ones self usually take precedence over other allegiances. Hence for any Nation to drop its guard economically, the way America did during the past 35-years, is highly idealistic. Such idealism and willingness to take risks, is the stuff political leadership is made of. But the risks are becoming too dangerous.

With the cold war diffused we can also wind-down our spending on armaments. That too will help level the playing field of economic competition.

Today's world is in rapid evolution politically economically and culturally. No it isn't revolution because no force of arms is involved, but it's happening faster than any revolution ever did.

During this exciting period in history, America finds itself in a quandary. It has held the free world's political leadership role, economic leadership role and cultural leadership role since the start of World War II. But drastic changes during the past decades have weakened America's position, particularly:

1) Our enormous budget deficits for Government as well as businesses and families,
2) Our growing trade deficit,
3) Our absence of adequate savings or profits for reinvestment in plant modernization or R&D, and
4) Our poor educational performance, leaving succeeding generations poorly prepared to inherit our debts.

Economic weakness causes political and cultural weakness. Only economic strength can recover what has been lost in political and cultural leadership. Hence America can focus the full force of its resources on economic recovery. The means for economic recovery clearly involve attitudinal changes as identified herein. These solutions for reversing America's decline, may be interpreted by some as too nationalistic or too protectionist. Neither is correct, as no unfair tariff barriers or trade barriers are involved! Encouraging Americans to freely choose American products at the cash register or to limit imports at an equal or lesser level than exported to each trading Nation, is not nationalistic or protectionist. It is realistic!

*Visualize a new American attitude* in which the "feeding frenzy" of mergers and buyouts, with associated price gouging in controlled markets, had stopped. Get-rich-quick speculators could then no longer legally "steal existing wealth" from unwary investors and savers. Imagine it being replaced by a system dependent on creating new wealth. The new wealth created in an expanding economy can readily create high paying jobs and rapidly pay off our debts, but first it will require Americans to make attitudinal changes about common values, such as by:

1) Being loyal buyers of products made in America by Americans.
2) Being demanding buyers who insist on innovation and quality.
3) Being austere buyers who only buy needed and functional products, not fads or impressive labels.
4) Being innovators and entrepreneurs who relish creativity and the enhancement of people's lives, thereby creating new wealth.
5) Being loyal employers who protect the interests of fellow Americans, such as by developing new technology in America for a "rolling-wave" of two years to create new jobs and new skills.
6) Being loyal employees who compete as dynamic individuals on behalf of your team's best interests.
7) Being savers rather than spenders.
8) Being investors, particularly on one's own creative new ideas starting new ventures.
9) Being trusting and trust worthy, so oral agreements and teamwork can replace litigious contracts and adversarial legal conflicts.
10) Being strong negotiators who seek to build a world economy can fairly evolve to new competitive levels, without damage to America's well-being.
11) Being faithful in the building of lasting relations with mates, children, family, friends and employees/employers.

12) Being communicative in forthrightly telling people what one thinks, so peers will know where you stand and act in accordance with that knowledge. Avoid apathy in all aspects of life.

13) Being focused on leaving behind this life a fullness of people who you helped and a sense of having contributed something of value to future generations.

In addition certain legislative action is warranted to enhance the effectiveness of people's changing attitudes. These surprisingly simple legislative actions can enhance America's competitive position and move towards implementation of New Ideas and New Ideals:

1) To encourage buying of American products, require labeling to identify the percentages owned and made in America.

2) To encourage long-range planning, provide investment tax credits for innovative new developments and modernization of existing plants.

3) To encourage research and creativity, hold competitions of significant monetary value and strengthen domestic and international patent laws.

4) To encourage exports, provide export tax credits.

5) Assimilate data from buyer's responses to a 2-month user questionnaire on most products, making it public in order to build a reliable statistical basis for the entrepreneurial development of new products.

6) To level-the-playing-field of international competition, require that each trading Nation raise their imports from us to the same quarterly value they desire to export to us.

7) To discourage litigation, require the loser to pay the winner's legal costs, with Government guarantees of payment if the loser's assets fall below a specified level. Also set limits of liability and hold-harmless protection for innovative products.

8) To enhance representative government, enable people to vote on issues when representative government's vote is too close to call, by dialing an (800) number.

9) To discourage terrorism declare an automatic state of war against all terrorist groups, wherever they may reside, if they act against United States citizens.

# VALUE #14: PEOPLE VALUES—Material Things vs. People

*By adopting values that emphasize giving to people and de-emphasize consumption of things, Americans can enhance their lives. Giving relationships, with both parties seeking to give of their own free will to satisfy each others needs without even being asked to do so, is the best way to strengthen marriages, families, friendships and business associations.*

What is wrong with our attitude and values in America? How can we change them to strengthen our Nation?

Today's societal values over-emphasize material possessions and de-emphasize people values. We use material wealth as the primary measure of success and respect, rather than the esteem in which family, friends and peers hold one. Individual pride and ego is focused on driving expensive cars and impressing friends with monetary success.

The pleasure of having material comforts and power is not wrong. Indeed it's a very positive motivator for working hard and striving for excellence and creativity. However self-indulgence and the satiation of needs can stop long before it does for many Americans. Pride and ego seem to continually call for more things and more services.

To refocus on people instead of things doesn't mean going without things. To live life fully is to live a balanced existence. Balance is needed both in the division of time and effort as well as the division of wealth. Full spectrums of opportunities are there for the taking. But seeking happiness and satisfaction through self-indulgence has become prevalent. To some the goal of life will continue to be satiation of their perceived desires. They will continue to "use" other people to satiate appetites for wealth, power, pride, status, ego and sexual desire. "Look on my works ye mighty and despair" was the poet's ridicule of such insatiable appetites, which are so fleeting in life.

Although none of us are selfless and few approach the level of a Mother Theresa or a Mahatma Ghandi, most people have a sense of public virtue and fairness. Most of us respond to moral issues, even when expedient solutions would be much easier and less costly. The world is in need of our public virtue because it's the best hope for Mankind to reach a universal sense of balance between the economic, social, political and environmental conflicts existing on planet Earth. Creating balance requires trade-offs be resolved between the value of people and the value of things.

*Visualize a new American attitude* in which individuals focus thinking on betterment of people as well as self-attainment of things. Too many live in loneliness because they concentrate on "Getting and spending. They lay waste their powers" (William Wordsworth), when judging success by material wealth.

Success is better judged by the esteem in which those who are closest hold one. Striving for material wealth and power in lieu of establishing close relationships is self-indulgent and a waste of life's precious time. People could instead derive their deepest satisfaction by accomplishing something of value, impacting on the well-being of people in current and future generations as well as their loved ones.

Ask yourself, is self-indulgence my own best interest as I evaluate all the options available to me? Is it in my own self-interest, even in the short term, to be dishonest and break mutual trusts? Is it in my own best interest to take from my spouse and not give back freely and openly? Is it in my own self-interest to give less than quality time in communicating with my children so their values about honor and shame are established, and they are encouraged to achieve? Is it in my own best interest to squander money and time on myself or might I be looking for more harmonious ways to use both?

What do we own in this life? What do we truly own? Certainly we have an indeterminate quantity of time living allots us from the moment of birth. At any period during this time, if we are lucky enough to evolve from childhood to old age, we own a certain amount of money and things as well as a certain amount of respect and affection from others in our lives.

That's it! That's what we own. We own a window of time on this Earth, during which money, things and peoples' respect pass through our life. How important are these material things we buy to please our sensory perceptions? How important is it to please our sense of smell by buying expensive perfumes? How important is it to buy expensive paintings to please our sense of sight? How important is it to buy expensive food to please our sense of taste? How important is it to please our sense of sound by buying expensive stereos? How important is it to be unfaithful to our spouses to please our sense of touch? How important is it to buy expensive cars to please our sense of pride, leaving our neighbors in awe?

Self-indulgence, by focusing on things to satiate our sense of power is a trap. It's a lifelong trap limiting true happiness by unbalancing our lives. True happiness requires an affirmative answer to fulfilling all of our sensory desires, in moderation and in harmony with one another. Each of us can seek to smell beautiful smells, taste wonderful food, see magnificent vistas, hear delightful music, touch the wonderful mate we have chosen for ourselves and read about new ideas. Sensory perceptions fulfill us in life and can be sought in competition.

Even pride and ego are real human objectives that can be nurtured, as long as we do so in harmony with other sources of happiness, particularly those pleasures coming from people in our lives. First and foremost, real happiness comes from people closest to us, spouse and children. Next it comes from family, friends, neighbors and business associates. Caring people give to others and receive commitments in return, having overwhelming value.

Commitment at the marital level can be sheer delight in the form of mutual adoration. To be adored by someone in a relationship is the highest honor one person can bestow on another. It's the total commitment of one person to another's well-being, without reservation or a negotiated demand for something in return.

When two people can achieve mutual adoration, giving to one another in all ways; monetarily, physically, emotionally, sensually and sexually; there is no stronger force on Earth for achieving happiness and harmony. A couple who can *give* to one another *without taking*, and *get* from one another *without demanding* it be given, has attained a high level of adoration. That is a root source of both pleasure and peace of mind in life.

This source of happiness is not limited to couples in intimate relationships. It's also applicable to friends who know the true meaning of friendship; such as friends who show up on moving day or painting day or cleaning day, roll up their sleeves and get to work without ceremony. Friends who can be counted on for such support are treasure money can't buy.

Even in business, happiness is to be found in relationships of trust. When we can count on a partner or business associate to think of our mutual best interest and accomplish tasks without being asked to do so, life becomes calm and pleasant.

Trust in a relationship is built on giving and getting, without taking, providing each partner with calm and steadfast support enhancing success in all areas of endeavor. Building such relationships can even enhance health and longevity.

A post-mortem analysis of a business, a friendship or a marriage can frequently be shown to involve vicious cycles of decline feeding on themselves. Consider a marriage in which the downhill cycle is only now starting with very minor points of dissension. Soon arguments begin and frustrations follow. This leads to negative actions, frequently involuntary (such as over-eating or over-smoking or over-drinking), building into a 2nd cycle of dissension. If over-drinking makes ones mate over-weight, a 3rd cycle may begin, such as infidelity. The vicious cycles then continue to degrade, until the relationship is severed with pain and anguish for all the family.

In marital relations, where trust and fidelity are too frequently challenged by promiscuity and lying to achieve sensory objectives, an in-depth evaluation can occur before taking action. A mate thinking to violate a lifelong commitment of trust usually can recognize the strife it will cause throughout many lives, and for many years. A trust once broken can never be fully repaired even if it is forgiven. In addition to the stress and strain of living with lies, fear of being caught can readily damage health. This eliminates calm and serenity, preventing the attainment of balance in one's life.

As a free people Americans individually have free will. We can wiggle our toes whenever we wish; proving no book of fate exists to limit our actions. Our freedom to act independent of the will of others makes us individually responsible for all actions we take in life. Hence our values with respect to time spent with people in our lives might become a conscious choice over self-indulgence.

## VALUE #15: INCOME TAX—Inequality vs. Equality

*By closing tax loopholes and stopping special interest lobbying for inequitable tax advantage, we can create a simple tax system having equality for all. A tax system based on a percentage of gross income, graduated to have the wealthy pay a higher percentage than the poor, would be both equitable and simple. It would eliminate tax inequities and close complex tax deduction loopholes for those wealthy enough to employ lobbyists.*

*A tax on gross income does not have to be a "flat-tax," which would continue the trickle-down theory of Voodoo economics. Causing all Americans to pay the same tax rate percentage of gross income would again benefit the wealthy and penalize most Americans.*

What is wrong with America's income tax regulations and tax legislation? How can we change them to strengthen our Nation?

America's income tax system has had ever increasing complexity added to it each year. Legislation favoring special interest lobbying groups result in tax regulations encouraging manipulation by experts who seek loopholes created by conflicting rules. The hodge-podge of legislation and regulations are too frequently linked to campaign contributions from special interest lobbying groups.

The use of wealth to influence tax legislation by campaign contributions and lobbying extends beyond Congress to State Legislations, County Boards of Supervisors and City Councils. Our current system *requires* elected officials to raise money from wealthy people, frequently permitting contributors to deduct contributions as legitimate expenses. In the highest income tax brackets, this is equivalent to having one-third of the campaign contributions lost to public coffers. By paying the other two-thirds out of public coffers, all voters could have an equal say to all elected officials.

*Visualize a new American attitude* in which influence peddling would be stopped in its tracks. A simple and equitable graduated tax on gross income would restore confidence in the American political system.

Apathy and despair are rampant today because trust has been jeopardized. Taxing gross income provides simplicity and equity because there are no deductions to manipulate and make complex.

Politicians have already recommended a tax on gross income but it has always been proposed as a flat-tax, wherein rich and poor pay the same tax rate percentage. Most Americans have been skeptical about the equity of a flat-tax rate. This could readily be overcome by graduating the percentage tax on gross income to reflect a system politically equitable to the American electorate.

Deductions for the benefit of society could continue on certain simply defined family issues, such as equal deductions for each child supported by a tax filing family or the cost of a child's education. The average annual cost for raising a child, say up to 18-years of age, could be made fully deductible as could other simply defined benefits to society.

## VALUE #16: INHERITANCE—Values vs. Wealth

*Inheritance can focus on giving and teaching equalitarian values to children, bringing happiness and joy to family life. Time spent together sharing life, gives both children and adults far more pleasure and wealth than does monetary inheritance after death. We can learn that an inheritance of thoughtful time spent together during life is far more significant than a eulogy of thanks for money saved as inheritance after life.*

*Accumulation of wealth for future generations has a negative value. There need be no limit on spending of earned wealth during anyone's lifetime, but also no monetary inheritance or monetary gifts from individual parents to their children or anyone else. All wealth would be liquidated on both parents' death, reverting their money to a common pool of inheritance for all children. Payments from this inheritance pool would be collected by Government and totally paid out each year, in equal portion, to all women and men as they start careers on their 18$^{th}$ birthday.*

What is wrong with our inheritance tax regulations and tax legislation in America? How can we change them to strengthen our Nation?

Recently four of the very richest men in America released a press statement condemning the Government for its plans to eradicate inheritance taxes. Warren Buffet, Bill Gates Sr., George Soros and Ted Turner spoke in favor of inheritance taxes. As the wealthiest men in America, they claimed charitable giving by the rich is largely based on choosing philanthropy over payment of Government income tax or inheritance tax. But tax incentives inhibit the joy of giving. They encourage tax avoidance of monies otherwise paid to Government. That is not the same joy derived from monies given freely, say to assist a friend's new business or a stranger's survival.

Many philanthropists, like Bernard Baruch donate because they believe it the right thing to do. Most need a reason to explain to their family heirs why they chose to "give away" any part of what the heirs think rightfully coming to them. Many family feuds start over inheritance, so what better way to avoid it than blame Government tax avoidance as the big bad bogeyman.

*Visualize a new American attitude* in which all wealth would be liquidated on both parents' death, reverting their money to a common pool of inheritance for all children. Payments from this inheritance pool would be collected by Government and totally paid out each year, in equal portion, to all women and men as they start careers on their 18$^{th}$ birthday.

Parents can savor earned wealth to enjoy their family's lives fully and give consumable benefits (such as education and health care) to their families and friends as they see fit. They can even give to strangers as contributions to art or charity.

As in board games we all played as children, such as Monopoly, American youth would start life on a level playing field with nearly equal financial resources. There would certainly be differences in the upbringing of children from wealthy families, but no disproportionate monetary assets at 18-years of age. How each youth chose to use their monetary resources to fulfill their lives, would be their individual challenge.

## VALUE #17: TERRORISM—Passive Acceptance vs. Active Response

*By taking hostage crucial facilities at the terrorist's home base, through air power, we can exert intense leverage on terrorists who will not want to do without strategic conveniences we hold hostage. No one need be killed on their side or ours.*

What is wrong with our attitude towards terrorism in America and how can we change it to strengthen our Nation?

Our weakness is we passively accept terrorism, whether by kidnapping Americans or by bombing airlines, terrorists know our rhetoric is usually followed by passive acceptance. Nationalistic fervor over centuries-old injustice is frequently accepted as reasonable. It is not! Such fervor should be reserved and maintained intense against only the living perpetrators. Later generations should not carry the burden of their forefather's injustices, making violence acceptable on a pretense of justice.

Legislation to fight terrorism with ground troops or swat teams is ineffective! American people do not wish to see another stream of body-bags as they witnessed in Vietnam. If Americans have finally concluded it's time to stop the nightmare of terrorism, a viable solution is available. To deal with terrorists from a position of strength we can use air power and sea power only, with no ground troops placed in harm's way.

*Visualize a new American attitude* in which the solution to terrorism lies in the art of negotiation. In any negotiation it's *leverage* which determines the outcome. Our leverage in dealing with terrorists today is negligible. To regain leverage, we as a Nation can agree on a policy. Any act of terrorism against a single American citizen can be declared an automatic "act of war" by the individual terrorist as well as any group sponsoring the act of aggression.

If a Nation is sponsoring the terrorists, we can diplomatically let that Nation know it has declared war on America. If the group is a terrorist cell (such as Hezzbollah or Osama bin Laden), harbored and nourished by a

Nation such as Libya, Iraq, Syria or Afghanistan, we should diplomatically let that Nation know we are at war. Let the world know we will not respect the territorial rights of any Nation harboring such terrorists.

To deal with terrorists from a position of strength (as in any good negotiation), requires taking hostage something they hold dear. However these need not and must not be innocent people's lives. Instead they can be *things*!

Our strength lies in air power and sea power. Only these can fight terrorism without many body-bags on either side. After a terrorist commits an act of aggression, it's appropriate for our Armed Forces to announce to the world we have taken hostages in retaliation. Not the terrorists or their families, whom they might consider expendable for their public relations cause, but rather the things they hold most dear such as:

o Arms Caches
o Training Camps and Headquarter Buildings
o Weapons and Equipment Installations
o Power Transmission Lines
o Telephone Lines
o Wireless and Internet Communication Towers
o Telephone Switching Stations
o Train Depots
o Truck Depots
o Power Plants and Switchyards
o Rail Lines
o Pipelines
o Airports
o Bridges
o Harbors
o Dams
o Water Sources and Water Treatment Plants
o Sewage Treatment Plants.

To exert leverage in a diplomatic negotiation is not to extract revenge; rather it is to make the price of continued terrorism so high terrorist's will cease and desist or move to another place. Hence our first step can be to drop multi-lingual leaflets throughout the terrorist's home base, wherever in the world that might be, identifying the specific targets from the above-listed sites which are to be destroyed in sequence. Each time there is evidence of who perpetrated a terrorist attack, bombing can begin within 10-days.

For example, with respect to hostages such as Terry Anderson and his companions, we Americans were guilty of criminal neglect. Hezzbollah committed an act of war, which the Government had no stomach to oppose. They could readily be extricated if America were willing to accept them as "prisoners of war." Once they are acknowledged as war prisoners, even though they are civilians, we can take the calculated risk of trying to free them by forceful negotiation.

What is "forceful negotiation?" It's negotiation with terrorists from a position of strength, even though risk is involved for harm to the hostages. Risk is always part of living and Americans can learn to deal with it better.

Step I in such a negotiation would have been to drop leaflets all around Beirut announcing the 50 facilities we are taking hostage with our air and sea power. To the extent possible, these sites should service the home base of Hezzbollah only. The leaflets would request all civilians to evacuate these sites within 10-days because one unnamed site will be demolished on day 11, unless all of the hostages are released unharmed. The leaflets would advise that unless all are released, another site of our selection would be demolished on each succeeding day. Should any one of the hostages not be released, the assumption will be made they have been martyred. Destruction will then continue until all 50 sites are destroyed. The taking of even one more hostage will be noted as cause for adding 20 more sites to the list.

Step II would consist of intensive diplomatic efforts to free all hostages during the 10-day grace period. No partial release should be tolerated.

Step III would be to again drop leaflets on day 10, narrowing the list of targets so civilians can evacuate safely but military defenses can not be installed to harm our pilots.

If on day 11 we must begin implementation—and it's doubtful we will have to–but then begin we must. Should the terrorists force civilians to remain at certain selected sites, we can have an alternate sequence of sites already planned from aerial surveillance. However the concern for civilians stops there. Civilians do die in war and the terrorists have declared the war.

Clearly this program does not "guarantee" the safe extrication of our hostages. However it's far more likely to bring them home unharmed than continued supplication or economic pressure. Terrorists may not be concerned for their own well being but their societies' peer pressure should cause them to cease and desist, rather than incur our wrath and losing the strategic facilities defined above. These are long-term losses of facilities, not rapidly replaced. Hopefully too high a price to pay for any short-term gains of terrorism.

# *About The Authors'*
# *And Their Objectives*

*AWAKEN AMERICA* is written to convey our thoughts and ideas for future relations between American people. As a couple married for 42-years since our high school courtship, we lived and traveled throughout America and firmly believe its people can build more powerful relations with one another.

Claiming no clairvoyance or prophecy, we hope *AWAKEN AMERICA* will help jump-start the individual process of stronger relations during the first century of the 3rd millennium. We believe women and men, of all religious beliefs and social customs can, during the next 100-years, evolve a common sense vision for forming and keeping democratic values of freedom, prosperity, intense competition without strife or war, personal creativity, innovation, political stability and environmental stability.

The authors base these hopes for future generations on two foundations of knowledge. We personally evaluated our own lives, including 47-years together, first in friendship and then in a loving and monogamous marriage. We also enjoyed our lifelong interest in history, especially America's rapidly changing democratic relations between women and men.

We observed a continuation of the system of patriarchy in our childhood during America's great depression and World War II. We were both exposed to the impacts of confusing values, weathering that emotional storm differently, until finding one another at 16-years of age. Now, after a lifelong friendship, we can better understand the confusion existing in America today.

We can look back on our lives together as a small part of history. We've observed and learned during our relationship including courtship, marriage, parenting, and grand-parenting, that vast opportunities exist for rapidly evolving much stronger relations between Americans. Knowing of vast differences existing between individual personalities and societal cultures, we desire to share that knowledge with others.

It's been our good fortune to live our lives together as Americans through the most exciting half-century since the beginning of time. It's been a half-century of strife and change, with far less war and killing than the prior half-century or any half-century before. It's been our good fortune to witness a beginning of the end for both the subjugation of American women and debilitation of its' men.

www.ingramcontent.com/pod-product-compliance
Lightning Source LLC
Chambersburg PA
CBHW061314280526
45784CB00002B/983